Secrets to Powerful Prayer

Discovering the Languages of the Heart

Secrets to Powerful Prayer

Discovering the Languages of the Heart

by
Lynne Hammond
and
Patsy Cameneti

Harrison House
Tulsa, Oklahoma

Secrets to Powerful Prayer
Discovering the Languages of the Heart
ISBN 1-57794-269-8
Copyright © 2000 by Lynne Hammond and Patsy Cameneti
P.O. Box 29469
Minneapolis, MN 55429

05 04 03 02 01   7 6 5 4 3 2

Published by Harrison House, Inc.
P.O. Box 35035
Tulsa, Oklahoma 74153

Contents

1

The Best Kind of Prayer

The effectual fervent prayer of
a righteous man availeth much.

JAMES 5:16

Almost two thousand years have passed since that Scripture was written, and during that time much has been said about prayer. Countless sermons have been preached about it. Multitudes of books have been written about it.

Yet with all we have learned about prayer, the bottom line still remains the same. It's the effectual fervent prayer that availeth. It's the prayer that brings the intended result that makes the difference. In other words, the best kind of prayer is the prayer that gets an answer.

Religion has tried to confuse the issue by saying things such as, "God always answers prayer, but sometimes the answer is *No.*" The Bible, however, doesn't say anything like that. According to the Bible, if you pray right you will receive what you ask for—every single time. God's answer to scriptural prayer is always Yes.

No doubt, that statement would upset some people. "Well, I don't think you can just expect God to do what you want Him to do every time you pray," they might say. "After all, He is a sovereign God and He does what He chooses."

Sure enough, He is a sovereign God. He does do what He chooses. And He has chosen to give us whatever we ask in Jesus' name. Jesus Himself said if those who believe Him would "ask anything" in His name, He would do it. (John 14:14.) He said in verse 13, **Whatsoever ye shall ask in my name, that will I do, that the Father may be glorified in the Son.**

Answered prayer isn't man's idea; it's God's idea.

Thus, when prayers aren't answered, it's not God's fault—it's ours. James 4:3 NKJV says, **You ask and do not receive, because you ask amiss.** When we don't receive what we pray for, either our motives or our methods are wrong. God's desire is for us to keep changing and keep learning until we grow to the place where we get everything we ask Him for.

How do I know that's possible?

Because Jesus received everything He asked for. And the Bible says we're destined to be just like Him. (Rom. 8:29.)

When Jesus prayed over the loaves and fishes, God answered and multiplied them to feed the thousands. When Jesus prayed for Lazarus to be raised from the dead, that's exactly what happened. When Jesus said to His disciples that He would pray the Father to send the Holy Ghost, God poured out His Spirit on the Day of Pentecost with the sound of a rushing mighty wind and tongues of fire.

Actually, every miracle in Jesus' life was born out of the time He spent in effectual prayer. The same will be true for us. As we learn to pray as He prayed, we'll do the works that He did—and even greater works. (John 14:12.)

Not Just an Opportunity, but a Responsibility

Truly, God has given us a wonderful part to play in His divine plan. By promising to answer our prayers, He has made it possible for us to become agents of His will on the earth. He's given us the privilege of making supernatural changes in natural circumstances. From our perspective, it is an amazing opportunity.

But God sees it as more than an opportunity; He considers it our responsibility. Read what Jesus said to His disciples in John 15:1-8,16 NKJV and you'll see what I mean.

"I am the True Vine, and My Father is the vinedresser. Every branch in Me that does not bear fruit He takes away; and every branch that bears fruit He prunes, that it may bear more fruit.

You are already clean because of the word which I have spoken to you. Abide in Me, and I in you. As the branch cannot bear fruit of itself, unless it abides in the vine, neither can you, unless you abide in Me.

I am the vine, you are the branches. He who abides in Me, and I in him, bears much fruit; for without Me you can do nothing. If anyone does not abide in Me, he is cast out as a branch and is withered; and they gather them and throw them into the fire, and they are burned.

If you abide in Me, and My words abide in you, you will ask what you desire, and it shall be done for you. By this My Father is glorified, that you bear much fruit; so you will be My disciples.

You did not choose Me, but I chose you and appointed you that you should go and bear fruit, and that your fruit should remain, that whatever you ask the Father in My name He may give you."

According to that last verse, our mission and purpose on this earth as Jesus' disciples is to bear fruit. What kind of fruit? The fruit of answered prayer! If we're not praying effective prayers that produce results, we're not fulfilling our purpose for being here. The reason we weren't beamed up to heaven as soon as we were born again is so we could pray and bear fruit for God!

One well-known minister said many years ago that it seems God will do nothing on the earth unless someone prays. Why is that? It's because, as Psalm 115:16 says, **The heaven, even the heavens, are the Lord's: but the earth hath he given to the children of men.** God gave authority on this earth to mankind, and through His mercies and grace, He desires to do great and wonderful things in and among people. He waits for a man or a woman to ask Him. He waits for someone to pray.

It's As Natural As Breathing

One reason Christians haven't taken up this great opportunity and responsibility as we should have is because we've allowed the Devil and religious tradition to convince us that prayer is hard. We've thought that prayer had to be dry and tedious and unrewarding. But that's a lie!

The truth is, prayer is a delightful thing for every true child of God because it takes us into the presence of our Father. What Isaiah prophesied in Isaiah 56:7 NKJV has come to pass for us. **"Even them I will bring to My holy mountain, and make them joyful in My house of prayer. Their burnt offerings and their sacrifices will be accepted on My altar; for My house shall be called a house of prayer for all nations."**

Prayer is not hard for those who have been born again into the family of God. It's a joy! Prayer comes as naturally to us spiritually as breathing does physically. True prayer rises naturally from the hearts of those who are joined to Jesus. It is an expression of a personal and intimate relationship with God. Such prayer doesn't have to be eloquent to be pleasing to the Lord. It just has to be sincere.

Have you ever seen a family gather around a baby who's just learning to talk? That baby doesn't have to say much to bring great joy to those who love him. He can babble something unintelligible and everyone—mom and dad, brothers and sisters, aunts and uncles—will rejoice over his efforts to communicate. "Oh, isn't he cute!" they'll say. "Isn't he smart?"

How much more does your heavenly Father rejoice over the words that rise to Him from the hearts of the children He so dearly loves? Just think how pleased He is when His children reach out to communicate with Him!

In the same way that a baby grows in his ability to communicate with his parents as he matures and keeps practicing those communications, so our ability to pray grows and develops the more we pray. Although studying books can help, we really learn how to pray by doing it.

Doing it is not a great strain or effort either, if we'll just stay fully connected to Jesus. Think again about what Jesus said in John 15:5,7 AMP. **I am the Vine, you are the branches. Whoever lives in Me and I in him bears much (abundant) fruit. If you live in Me—abide vitally united to Me—and My words remain in you and continue to live in your hearts, ask whatever you will and it shall be done for you.**

When we're living in vital union with Jesus, praying effective prayers comes from us just as naturally and easily as fruit grows on the branch of a vine. Have you ever seen a branch straining, grimacing and saying, "Come on, fruit...grow, grow, grow"? Of course not. That branch simply does what it does naturally, by virtue of the life that flows to it from the vine.

It's important to understand, however, that living in vital union with Jesus means more than just being born again. As Christians, we all have a connection to Jesus. But we can all look back over our lives and realize there were some times when we were more strongly in union with Him than we were at other times.

If you've ever seen a tree with a broken branch, you know that if it isn't broken completely, a single connection to the tree will keep it alive. There won't be enough life there, however, for the branch to bear fruit. In the same way, if your fellowship with God is broken because you haven't been walking with Him in accordance with His Word, that doesn't change your position of righteousness. You are still a righteous branch, but there probably won't be enough life coming from your connection with God to enable you to bear fruit.

Being vitally united to God will bring you to a place where all you ask will be granted because, when you are in full union with Him, everything that is in you comes from Him. When you are vitally united with Him, you'll want what He wants. You'll have in your heart what He has in His heart. Therefore, your prayers will be His prayers. And you can be sure He will answer every prayer that originates with Him.

That just makes good sense! God would never initiate a prayer He does not intend to answer. The prayer that's started in Him will be finished in Him.

Attend to the Word

How do you maintain that kind of vital union with Jesus? Once again, look at John 15:7 AMP: **If My words remain in you and continue to live in your hearts, ask whatever you will and it shall be done for you.**

You might have a deep hunger for God, but if you don't attend to His Word, you will not be vitally united with Him. If you fail to feed on the Word of God—reading, studying, meditating on it and obeying it—your prayer life will be weak and ineffective. If you want a powerful, effective prayer life, you must spend enough time in the Word of God for it to come alive in you.

George Mueller, a tremendous man of God, spent days poring over the Word of God. Sometimes he would study what the Word had to say about something for two weeks before he prayed about it. Then, when he prayed, he kept the Bible open before him.

I prayed with an older woman for several years who was much the same way. She was so full of the Word of God and she had gotten it so deeply into her heart, that it would come out of her mouth with tremendous power when she prayed. That Word became a sword slicing through the Devil's schemes and bringing forth the will of God. I've never known anyone who could use the Word of God like she did. As she would yield herself to the Holy Spirit in prayer, she would use verses from the Bible in the most unusual and amazing ways. I'm telling you, when she said, "It is written," the Devil got out of her way!

Now, someone else might say, "It is written," and it might not impress the Devil one bit. He knows what is written, and it doesn't bother him when people quote the Bible. Too often, that's what Christians do. They just repeat scriptural words that aren't really alive to them. They speak the Word, but they're not really believing it because they haven't spent enough time meditating on it to move into a place of faith.

When the Word of God is alive to you, when it is more real to you than the natural world around you, your prayers are effective. When you've stored up that Word within you, the Holy Spirit can quicken it to you and show you how to pray it out. But you have to give Him something to work with. You have to have the Word of God, not just in books and on tapes and in Bibles on your coffee table. You have to have it living in your heart!

The best kind of prayer, the kind that always brings results, is the kind of prayer that comes from a believer who's full of the Word of God and responsive to the Spirit of God. The Lord has been looking for people who would pray like that for a long time. In John 4:23-24 NKJV, Jesus said,

> "The hour is coming, and now is, when the true worshipers will worship the Father in spirit and truth; for the Father is seeking such to worship Him.
>
> God is Spirit, and those who worship Him must worship in spirit and truth."

When the Holy Spirit is joined with the Word of God, the result is always powerful, effective prayer.

All Kinds of Prayer

One of the things the Word reveals to us is that there are many different kinds of prayer. In Ephesians 6:18 NKJV, the apostle Paul said we should pray **always with all prayer and supplication in the Spirit, being watchful to this end with all perseverance and supplication for all the saints.** The Amplified translation of that verse says **to pray with all manner of prayer.**

In sports there are all kinds of games: baseball, basketball, football, soccer and golf, to name a few. Making a touchdown will not score you any points in golf, and the same generally is true in prayer. Applying the wrong kind of prayer to a given situation will not bring the desired results.

So to help us pray more effectively, in the chapters ahead we'll dig into the Word of God and study three general categories of prayer. The first category is prayer that changes things. Within that category we will take an in-depth look at the prayer of agreement, the prayer of binding and loosing, the prayer of faith, the prayer of petition, intercessory prayer and united prayer.

The second category includes prayers of thanksgiving and praise. The third involves prayers of dedication and consecration.

As you learn more of what the Bible has to say about these kinds of prayers, you'll give the Holy Spirit more to work with as He leads you into a lifestyle of answered prayer.

2

Casting Your Cares

*Therefore humble yourselves...under the mighty
hand of God, that in due time He may exalt you.
Casting the whole of your care—all your anxieties,
all your worries, all your concerns, once and for
all—on Him; for He cares for you affectionately,
and cares about you watchfully.*

1 Peter 5:7 AMP

Because of its importance, the first kind of prayer we want
to examine is the prayer of casting your cares upon the
Lord. Through this type of prayer, you can take everything
that's worrying you, tie it all up in a bundle and give it to God.
You can take your cares to His throne, leave them with Him,
trusting Him to deal with them for you, and walk away from
them completely carefree.

The reason we must learn this kind of prayer first is simple. If you don't know how to pray this prayer, many of your other prayers will be rendered ineffective. That's because every effective prayer you will ever pray must be based on your faith in the Word of God. And Jesus warned us in Matthew 13:22 that the worries and cares of this world will choke out the Word you've put in your heart.

Let's say, for example, that you've been praying for your child. You've based your prayer on Isaiah 54:13 that says, **All thy children shall be taught of the Lord; and great shall be the peace of thy children.**

The more you meditate on that Word, the stronger your faith becomes. You are praying effective prayers because you have an inner image of that Word coming to pass in your child's life. In your heart, you see him learning from God, serving Him and living a peaceful, godly life.

But then, let's say, your child gets into some trouble. Maybe he starts running around with the wrong kinds of kids. You have some genuine concern about the problems he's creating for Himself, so you start to worry. Before you know it, you're walking around wringing your hands and thinking, *Oh my, if that boy doesn't straighten up, he's going to end up getting involved with drugs. He's going to end up in jail. He's going to end up throwing his whole life away.*

The more you worry, the less power the Word will have on your thoughts. Like Jesus said, those cares will come up like weeds and thorns and choke out that inner image of Isaiah 55 and replace it with an image of that child in jail.

Fear will strangle your faith, and your prayers for your child will become powerless.

When you understand that devilish progression, you'll see why Jesus so strongly admonished us not to worry. He didn't make it a suggestion. He made it a command, because when you worry, you're giving the Devil the place in your life that the Word is supposed to have. You are meditating on his power to hurt you instead of meditating on God's power to deliver you.

In Luke 21:34 NKJV, Jesus was talking to His disciples about the day of His return, and He said, **Take heed to yourselves, lest your hearts be weighed down with carousing, drunkenness, and cares of this life, and that Day come on you unexpectedly.**

Jesus knew that if they let worry overtake them, they could miss out on the time of their visitation and not be ready for His Second Coming. The same is true for us. We can miss out on God's presence and power in our lives. We can miss out on the day of our deliverance. How? By being so focused on a problem Satan has presented us with that we take our eyes off God and become unaware of what He is doing.

Again in Matthew 6:25-34 NKJV, Jesus gave us this important charge:

> **"Therefore I say to you, do not worry about your life, what you will eat or what you will drink; nor about your body, what you will put on. Is not life more than food and the body more than clothing?**

Look at the birds of the air, for they neither sow nor reap nor gather into barns; yet your heavenly Father feeds them. Are you not of more value than they?

Which of you by worrying can add one cubit to his stature? So why do you worry about clothing? Consider the lilies of the field, how they grow: they neither toil nor spin; and yet I say to you that even Solomon in all his glory was not arrayed like one of these.

Now if God so clothes the grass of the field, which today is, and tomorrow is thrown into the oven, will He not much more clothe you, O you of little faith? Therefore do not worry, saying, 'What shall we eat?' or 'What shall we drink?' or 'What shall we wear?' For after all these things the Gentiles seek. For your heavenly Father knows that you need all these things.

But seek first the kingdom of God and His righteousness, and all these things shall be added to you.

Therefore do not worry about tomorrow, for tomorrow will worry about its own things. Sufficient for the day is its own trouble."

It's no wonder that in this passage we are told five times, "Do not worry." Not only is worry absolutely useless, it does harm to your prayer life and your physical well-being.

Satan understands this principle so he purposefully creates situations to make you worry. For him, it's an easy and effective way to neutralize your prayers. But you can defeat that strategy by learning to take those worries to God in prayer and cast them over onto Him.

It's Not Irresponsible

❦

But wait a minute, you may be thinking. *Isn't it irresponsible just to ignore your troubles by not worrying about them?*

If all you did was ignore them, it would be irresponsible. We've all known people who've done that. They deal with problems by just choosing not to think about them. They don't worry about where they're going to live because they figure they'll live off someone else. That is not what we're talking about.

We're talking about taking a situation which you are unable to do anything about and putting it in the hands of the Someone who is able to do something about it. Through prayer, you are going to give that problem to the only One who has the power to solve it. And that's the most responsible thing you can do.

There may be other people who are concerned about your finances, but they may not have the money or the desire to meet your need. God has both. Someone may be very sorry that you are facing a serious illness, but they aren't the healer. God is the healer, and He's ever ready to heal you.

Of course, before you can confidently take your cares to Him, you must have the assurance that God is trustworthy. Maybe you've had some disappointing experiences with people in the past. Maybe you trusted them to take care of something for you and they forgot or let you down. Before you can cast your cares completely on God, you must be sure He won't take them today and forget about them tomorrow. You must be certain He won't say, "Oops, sorry. Yesterday was a busy day. I had so many things on My mind that I lost track of your concerns in the shuffle."

How can you gain that reassurance? You go to the Bible and remind yourself of His faithfulness and power. Go to verses that remind you of God's care and concern for you. Meditate on Scriptures like Hebrews 13:5 AMP: **For He (God) Himself has said, I will not in any way fail you nor give you up nor leave you without support. [I will] not, [I will] not, [I will] not in any degree leave you helpless, nor forsake nor let [you] down [relax My hold on you]—Assuredly not!**

Think about Romans 4:21 AMP that says God is **able and mighty to keep His word and to do what He had promised.** Or Psalm 34:19 AMP that says, **Many evils confront the [consistently] righteous; but the Lord delivers him out of them all.**

It's important that you meditate on such Scriptures before you pray the prayer of casting your cares because you don't want this prayer to be just a form. You want to pray it from your heart. You want it to be the real deal.

Have you ever been burdened by a problem and had someone flippantly say to you, "Oh, well, just cast it on the Lord?" You may have smiled and agreed on the outside, but on the inside you were thinking, *Yeah, that's easy for you to say!*

You might have even gone through the motions of prayer with that person. But it was a plastic prayer because you never actually connected with God in your heart about the matter.

You had no clear, scriptural confidence that God could or would handle the problem and, as a result, there was no genuine transaction between Him and you. So as that person walked away gaily, saying, "Now, just praise the Lord till it's done!" you were still knotted up inside, wondering, *What on earth am I going to do?*

I had a woman come to me once who was facing a very real and difficult problem. She wasn't overreacting to a little thing; she was up against something very big. She had natural reason to worry. I knew that before I could pray with her, I needed to help her cast the care of it on the Lord. So we went over some Scriptures and I reminded her of what God said He would do about this situation.

It doesn't bother God that we need to have constant reassurance that He is qualified to take our burdens. He wants us to have that reassurance. That's why He gave us His Word with all its glorious promises. He put Himself on paper so we could learn of His character.

In addition to what the Bible said, that dear lady and I discussed what I had seen God do in my life and in the lives of many others. She began to get more and more calm. Then, from her heart, she gave that problem to the Lord. A week later I heard how wonderfully God had moved on her behalf.

When someone comes to you in distress and needs prayer, remember that it's not enough just to get them to quit crying and then say to them, "Don't worry! Cast your cares on the Lord!" Help them do it. Give them some promises from the

Word of God that will inspire faith in them. Faith is a real substance. It will strengthen them and comfort them.

Be prepared to stick with them for a while. Sometimes it takes people a little time to grasp the fact that God really will help them. Don't try to get them to turn loose of their care before then. As you feed on the Word with them, they will begin to relax. You can tell when the Word has broken through their fears and they are focusing on God instead of the problem. At that point, have them begin to pray and they'll be able to truly cast their cares upon the Lord.

A Four-Part Prayer

Philippians 4:6-8 NKJV gives us very practical insight into how we pray this prayer of casting your care.

> Be anxious for nothing, but in everything by prayer and supplication, with thanksgiving, let your requests be made known to God; and the peace of God which surpasses all understanding, will guard your hearts and minds through Christ Jesus.

> Finally, brethren, whatever things are true, whatever things are noble, whatever things are just, whatever things are pure, whatever thing are lovely, whatever things are of good report, if there is any virtue and if there is anything praiseworthy—meditate on these things.

The first word I want you to notice there is the word *supplication*. To supplicate means more than just to ask someone for something. It implies that you are pouring your heart out about something that you need.

Therefore, to effectively pray the prayer of casting your care, you must do more than just say something general, such as, "Lord, I give all my worries to You. Amen." You must get specific. Tell the Lord exactly what cares you are asking Him to take, and tell Him everything that's been bothering you about them.

In other words, *unload* on Him.

If you've ever had another person unload on you, you know what that's like. They don't just say, "I had a bad day." They give you all the gory details. They tell you what happened. They tell you how they felt about it. They take everything that's inside them and pour it out on you.

That's exactly the way you cast your cares upon the Lord. You stop trying to sound all nice and spiritual, and you just have a conversation with God and tell Him everything that's been worrying you.

Once you've done that, make a definite request. Ask Him to meet your need, give you wisdom or simply handle the problem. Don't be nebulous. Be definite with God. Say, "Lord, this is the amount of money I need. I don't care how You bring it. All I know is that You said, they that love the Lord will not want for any good thing. (Ps. 34:10.) So I trust You, and I'm asking You to provide."

Whenever I'm having trouble with worry, I set aside a specific time and place to get it all out. Then when the Devil comes back to me and tries to get me all upset about that situation again, I can refuse him. I'll say, "No, I won't take that back. I remember exactly when and where I was when I gave that to God. I told Him everything that was bothering me about that situation. Now it belongs to Him, and I won't touch it with worry."

Some people might think it's arrogant to say something like that. They might feel it's presumptuous just to tell God what you need and expect Him to take care of it. But it's not. On the contrary, casting your care on God is an act of humility. First Peter 5:6-7 AMP bears that out. It says, **Humble yourselves ...under the mighty hand of God...casting the whole of your care...on Him.** When you pray this prayer, you are demonstrating the fact that you believe God is bigger than you are, that He is able to fix this problem. You are admitting that you are totally dependent upon Him.

After you've settled things with God by making a definite request, the next thing you need to do is thank Him. I realize you haven't seen results in the natural realm yet, but your faith isn't based on what you see; it's based on what you believe. And you should be believing 1 John 5:14-15 NKJV.

> **Now this is the confidence that we have in Him, that if we ask anything according to His will, He hears us. And if we know that He hears us, whatever we ask, we know that we have the petitions that we have asked of Him.**

According to this passage, if we ask knowing that God hears us, we can have absolute confidence that we have our answer. That is reason enough to give thanks!

After you thank God for taking care of your situation, if you've really prayed from your heart, you'll notice a supernatural peace begin to settle over you. That's the divine order of things: prayer first, thanksgiving second and peace third. You can never rearrange or change that progression.

There may be times when someone will come to you literally shaking with anxiety and ask you to pray for them. You can pray for the peace of God to come upon them. You can ask for the Prince of Peace to comfort them. But if that person is worried about a specific situation, those prayers won't help them. You'll have to lead them the biblical way.

Prayer, supplication and thanksgiving: that's the way to peace. There are no shortcuts that will get you there by a quicker route.

So when someone comes to you for prayer, ask them specifically what's bothering them. Then, as they begin to unburden themselves, you might say, "Wait a minute. Why don't you just tell all this to God? Telling me won't help you very much, but telling Him will."

They may be uncomfortable at first because that kind of praying doesn't sound very spiritual. But encourage them to talk to Him just like they were talking to you. Then they'll be able to cast those cares on Him and experience the peace they so desperately need.

Once we find that peace, we maintain it by obeying the fourth part of that passage in Philippians 4. We fix our minds on what the Word of God says is true about our situation. We think good and praiseworthy things.

When worry comes knocking at your door, turn it away and choose to meditate on thoughts of faith instead. When you've prayed about that child according to Isaiah 55 and then he gets in trouble, don't start thinking about that trouble. Instead, fix your mind on what the Bible says. Say to yourself, "Bless God, that child is a child of the righteous, and he is a disciple of the Lord. I don't care what the Devil tries to do to draw that kid into sin, it isn't going to work. He's going to end up living for the Lord. He's going to end up victorious and prosperous and blessed because God is faithful, and He told me that's how things are going to be."

It's important that you understand I'm not suggesting you just suppress your fears by refusing to think about them. No, you've gotten rid of those fears by casting them over on God and replacing them with faith. You are simply refusing to allow those fears to come back by shutting the door on them. You continue to keep them out by keeping your mind and your heart full of the Word of God.

As you do, you'll continue to pray powerful prayers, prayers unhindered by worry and care. Prayers that get results.

3

The Prayer of Consecration

"...I have been crucified with Christ;
it is no longer I who live, but Christ
lives in me; and the life which I now live
in the flesh I live by faith in the Son of God,
who loved me and gave Himself for me."

GALATIANS 2:20 NKJV

The prayer of consecration may be one of the shortest prayers ever uttered, but it often requires the longest journey of the heart. It is not fun to die to our own will and our own ways. And that's what it takes to surrender to God's will and His ways. That's what it takes to honestly pray this kind of prayer.

The best scriptural example of the prayer of consecration is found in Matthew 26:36-46 NKJV.

Then Jesus came with them to a place called Gethsemane, and said to the disciples, "Sit here while I go and pray over there."

And He took with Him Peter and the two sons of Zebedee, and He began to be sorrowful and deeply distressed. Then He said to them, "My soul is exceedingly sorrowful, even to death. Stay here and watch with Me."

✳ He went a little farther and fell on His face, and prayed, saying, "O My Father, if it is possible, let this cup pass from Me; nevertheless, not as I will, but as You will."

Then He came to the disciples and found them sleeping, and said to Peter, "What? Could you not watch with Me one hour? Watch and pray, lest you enter into temptation. The spirit indeed is willing, but the flesh is weak."

Again a second time, He went away and prayed, saying, "O My Father, if this cup cannot pass away from Me unless I drink it, Your will be done."

And He came and found them asleep again, for their eyes were heavy. So He left them, went away again, and prayed the third time, saying the same words. Then He came to His disciples and said to them, "Are you still sleeping and resting? Behold, the hour is at hand, and the Son of Man is being betrayed into the hands of sinners. Rise, let us be going. See, My betrayer is at hand."

This prayer, with all its intensity, didn't just spontaneously spring up in Jesus' heart at this one crucial time in His life. Although this Garden of Gethsemene experience was the ultimate test of His willingness to die to His own will, Jesus lived His entire life with this attitude of surrender to God.

In John 5:30 NKJV, He said, **I can of Myself do nothing. As I hear, I judge; and My judgment is righteous, because I do not seek My own will but the will of the Father who sent Me. And again in John 6:38 NKJV, He said, For I have come down from heaven, not to do My own will, but the will of Him who sent Me.**

This was Jesus' own testimony. Choosing God's will over His own was the most important thing in His life.

Desiring the Better Part

An interesting thing happens to us when we surrender our lives to the lordship of Jesus and receive the baptism in the Holy Spirit. Over time our desires change so that we begin desiring what God desires. To a great extent, our personal will merges with God's will, and we naturally want to do what He wants us to do.

I don't spend every day torn between the desire to work in a casino and the desire to teach the Word of God. I never have a day when I say, "Oh, I can't decide if I want to serve the Lord or deal drugs." No, my desires and God's desires have merged together so that everything in me wants to serve the Lord.

Yet, even so, there are times when a conflict will arise. There are times when my soul will want to go one way and the

Holy Spirit will direct me to go another. There are times when God will ask me to do something for Him that will cost me something personally. At those times, my natural self will want to fight against God's instructions. It will say, "Hey, I don't want to do that. It's going to hurt!"

When that happens, I have a choice to make. Am I going my way or God's way?

For me, the worst thing I could possibly imagine is to stand before the Lord one day and hear Him tell me, "Well half done. You started off good, but you missed My plan for your life." So in those circumstances, I pray the prayer of consecration. I say, "Not my will, Lord, but Yours be done."

Finish the Course

One of the reasons the prayer of consecration is so important is that we all face choices like that—not just once, but again and again. So this isn't a prayer you can pray once in your life. It has to be prayed continually. It has to be the rudder that directs your course.

Paul said in 2 Timothy 4:7, **I have fought a good fight, I have finished my course, I have kept the faith.**

The course that Paul was referring to was the will of God for his life. Each and every one of us has a course to run. Hebrews 12:1 NKJV says, **Therefore we also, since we are surrounded by so great a cloud of witnesses, let us lay aside every weight,**

and the sin which so easily ensnares us, and let us run with endurance the race that is set before us.

The Amplified translation says that we are to run our **appointed course.** That means my course won't be the same as yours. Your course won't be the same as someone else's. All of our courses are different, because God has a different plan for each of our lives.

Picture a road that winds and turns from the time you surrendered your will to Jesus to the end where you finish your course. That road represents the will of God for your life. It will bend and turn and go to all kinds of exciting places. There will be different things along your course that try to pull you off the road. It could be a business opportunity or a relationship that beckons you. But there is only one way to reach the end of your course, and that is to seek out and follow the will of God.

Don't Hold Your Life Dear

Paul was talking about all the things that were trying to get him off his course in Acts 20:24 NKJV when he said, **But none of these things move me; nor do I count my life dear to myself, so that I may finish my race with joy, and the ministry which I received from the Lord Jesus, to testify to the gospel of the grace of God.**

First, he said that none of those things moved him. Second, he said that he did not count his life dear. If you hold your life dear, mark it down—you're not going to finish your course. If it means everything to you to have a good reputation, don't plan on finishing your course because the Devil will set a trap to make you popular. If it means a lot to you to have a nice house, you'll probably get one, but forget about finishing your course. Forget about hearing the words, "Well done," because the Devil will provide a way of getting you a nice house that will be guaranteed to get you off your course.

Does that mean you can't have a nice home and still finish your course? No, not at all. But if a house means *more* to you than God's will, you'll jump up and accept the enemy's plan rather than wait with patience for God's plan.

If you can be snagged by money, don't plan on finishing your course. That doesn't mean you have to run your race in poverty. God wants you to prosper. And if you'll serve Him in faith, He will bless you financially. But if you love money, the Devil will use it to lure you off track. He'll make you an offer you can't refuse, and you'll end up saying, "Not Your will, Lord, but mine be done."

Nothing is as high as the call of God. Yet I've seen single people make marriage their prize and high calling. They will fight, claw and scratch to get a marriage relationship. Then, when they get it, they despise it because it cost them the peace of living out of the plan of God.

Small Steps to Gethsemane

❧

Jesus didn't develop the Gethsemane attitude of consecration overnight. Many small steps of surrender paved the way for that final decision, and you'll have to take a lot of small steps in your life, too. You will have daily opportunities for consecration when somebody wrongs you, and God tells you to bless them instead of giving them a piece of your mind. You'll take small steps forward on those days when you want to go home and relax after a hard day and God tells you instead to go to the church and pray.

There will also be big steps of consecration along the way. When you are offered a chance to fulfill your dream but God directs you another way, for instance, what will you do? If you've practiced the prayer and the attitude of consecration, you'll make the right decision. You'll turn down that *good* opportunity and wait for a *God* opportunity instead.

To make choices like that, your love for God has to be in first place. You must simply trust that surrendering to His will for you will take you to the highest possible kind of life. You must believe that His plan will eventually be much better than what you could have gotten on your own.

I'll warn you now, there will be occasions when you have a dream in your heart that God Himself put there, but the direction He is leading you seems to be taking you away from that dream instead of toward it. Don't worry about that. Just keep walking with God. I can't tell you how many times I've thought, *What does this job have to do with what's in my heart?* The answer, of course, is everything. There are people who are not doing the will of God for their life, because they're too busy trying to fulfill their God-given dreams in their own human way.

Sometimes you have to die to those dreams to stay on course. (Remember when God told Abraham to sacrifice Isaac?) But if you'll do it, God will surely resurrect that dream at the right time and in the right way.

At those times of consecration, you learn like the apostle Paul did not to count your life dear to yourself. Remember, however, that doesn't mean that God does not hold your life dear. He holds it so dear that He shed His own blood for it. So trust Him to do something with your life. If you will, He will surely give you the desires of your heart.

Delight in God

Of course, those kinds of dying-to-self decisions hurt in the short run. But that's okay because every time you make a decision that hurts—perhaps you decide against a relationship, a business or some other opportunity—you're making a long-term investment toward God's plan for your life. The more it costs you now to follow God's plan, the less likely you'll be to let something cheap pull you off your course later. God's plan is more valuable than anything else in life. That's why consecration, though sometimes painful, is not a negative thing. It will endear the will of God to your life. It will cause you to treat it as the precious treasure that it is.

Notice that when Paul said in Acts 20:24 NKJV that he didn't count his life dear, he talked about two distinct things: his race and the ministry. **But none of these things move me; nor do I count my life dear to myself, so that I may finish my race with joy, and the ministry which I received from the Lord Jesus, to testify to the gospel of the grace of God.**

He wanted to finish his course and his ministry. They aren't the same thing! Your course isn't just ministry; it involves many things. One key to completing your course is being joyful every step of the way. You'll never get further down the road if you despise where you are. If the only thing you have to be happy about is that you're in the will of God—that's enough! "Praise God, I'm on my course!" Learn to delight in the scenery around you, and you'll learn to delight in the will of the Lord even if it takes you through the jungles in Afghanistan. Delighting in the Lord will bring divine appointments.

God Wants You To Be Strong-Willed

Before you reach the end of your course, you'll learn to be very good at the prayer of consecration and dedication. Three times in Matthew 26, Jesus asked that the cup pass from Him. But He didn't stop there. He added, **Nevertheless, not as I will, but as thou wilt.**

God does not take us through the consecration process to cause us to lose our will. He does not want you to be without a will. If that had been His intent, He would never have created you with one. Truthfully, by the time you finish your course, you'll be very strong-willed. But your will always will be used to fulfill God's will.

Jesus didn't want to have nails hammered in His hands and feet. His flesh didn't want to die. Everything in Him drew back, but when He prayed the prayer of consecration—"not as I will"—He became very strong-willed. Strong enough to endure the cross.

James 4:13-15 NKJV admonishes us to consecrate every day to the will of God.

> Come now, you who say, "Today or tomorrow we will go to such and such a city, spend a year there, buy and sell, and make a profit"; whereas you do not know what will happen tomorrow. For what is your life? It is even a vapor that appears for a little time and then vanishes away.
>
> Instead you ought to say, "If the Lord wills, we shall live and do this or that."

Don't just exercise your will in big things. Practice the prayer of consecration daily. It will keep you conscious that God has a plan for you.

The following are a few scriptural prayers of consecration you can pray:

> For this reason we also, since the day we heard it, do not cease to pray for you, and to ask that you may be filled

with the knowledge of His will in all wisdom and spiritual understanding; that you may walk worthy of the Lord, fully pleasing Him, being fruitful in every good work and increasing in the knowledge of God; strengthened with all might, according to His glorious power, for all patience and longsuffering with joy; giving thanks to the Father who has qualified us to be partakers of the inheritance of the saints in the light.

COLOSSIANS 1:9-12

Teach me to do Your will, for You are my God; Your Spirit is good. Lead me in the land of uprightness.

PSALM 143:10 NKJV

"I delight to do Your will, O my God, and Your law is within my heart."

PSALM 40:8 NKJV

[Not in your own strength] for it is God Who is all the while effectually at work in you—energizing and creating in you the power and desire—both to will and to work for His good pleasure and satisfaction and delight."

PHILIPPIANS 2:13 AMP

Praying these Scriptures will help you start turning your heart in the right direction. At times, even as you pray them, your soul may be making you miserable with thoughts of how hard it's going to be to obey God in a certain circumstance. If so, be honest with God about it. Jesus was. He said, **"My soul is exceedingly sorrowful"** (Matt. 26:38). God won't mind your being in His throne room, saying, "Oh, God, I want to do Your will, but my soul hurts."

Once you consecrate yourself, don't stop there. Learn to get on your face before God until you know exactly what His will for you is. Then, the next time you come to a crossroads in your life, pray the prayer of consecration.

And finish your course.

4

~~~

United Prayer

*And when they heard...they lifted up their
voice to God with one accord and said....*

ACTS 4:24

When we as believers come together collectively in united
prayer, the Spirit of the Lord moves among us. We
experience a fullness of the Spirit that cannot be obtained by
any other kind of prayer. United prayer brings powerful results.
It doesn't just change the life of one individual, it affects entire
groups of people. Real united prayer can affect an entire
church, city, state or even a nation. It creates an open heaven
where there is no opposition in the spirit realm and clears the
way for God to move freely.

Great things happen under an open heaven. When the
heavens opened over Jacob in Genesis 28:13-14 NKJV, he saw

41

the Lord and received a blessing from Him that affected not just Jacob, but millions of his descendents. God said,

> "I am the Lord God of Abraham your father and the God of Isaac; the land on which you lie I will give to you and your descendants.
>
> Also your descendants shall be as the dust of the earth; you shall spread abroad to the west and the east, to the north and the south; and in you and in your seed all the families of the earth shall be blessed."

That is the result of an open heaven.

According to Mark 1:9-10, Jesus saw an open heaven when He came up out of the water after being baptized. **And straightway coming up out of the water, he saw the heavens opened, and the Spirit like a dove descending upon him: And there came a voice from heaven, saying, Thou art my beloved Son, in whom I am well pleased.**

If you continue reading, you'll find that after the heavens were opened, things began happening "immediately." Immediately a fever left. Immediately leprosy departed. Immediately he took up his bed and walked. It is clear that an open heaven provides immediate miracles.

Recently, when I was reading about a missionary who was working in the mountains of Brazil and Uruguay, I saw a wonderful example of what happens when people in a nation pray together and open the heavens. The border of the two nations ran down the center of the street, with Brazil on one side and Uruguay on the other. As the missionary began handing out tracts, he noticed something very powerful. On the Uruguayan side of the street, not one person took a tract. Not one. They would snub him and walk away. On the Brazililian side of the street, however, everyone took a tract and thanked him for it. After an hour, he saw a woman from the Uruguayan side of the street who had refused a tract walk across to the Brazilian side. He followed her across the street and tried to give her a tract again. This time she took it and said, "Thank you very much. I appreciate it."

Why did that happen? It was a direct result of opposition in the realm of the spirit over Uruguay, and an open heaven over Brazil. We need an open heaven, and the way to get one is to pray corporately in one accord. That's the reason Dr. David Cho is having so much success in Korea. He has an army of people who are powerful in prayer, and it has created an open heaven.

In Times of Crisis

In the Bible, we see four different kinds of situations where united prayer is necessary. The first is during a time of crisis.

If you've ever taken part in united prayer, you know that there is a real note of power that comes forth from it. That's why this is the prayer to pray in times of crisis. It accesses the power of God. You can see a demonstration of that in Acts 4:23-32, when the religious leaders threatened to hurt Peter and John unless they stopped preaching about Jesus. At that moment, the members of the early church were facing a crisis. What did they do?

> And being let go, [Peter and John] went to their own company, and reported all that the chief priests and elders had said unto them.

> And when they heard that, they lifted up their voice to God with one accord, and said, Lord, thou art God, which hast made heaven, and earth, and the sea, and all that in them is: Who by the mouth of thy servant David hast said, Why did the heathen rage, and the people imagine vain things?

> The kings of the earth stood up, and the rulers were gathered together against the Lord, and against his Christ.

> For of a truth against thy holy child Jesus, whom thou hast anointed, both Herod, and Pontius Pilate, with the Gentiles, and the people of Israel, were gathered together, for to do whatsoever thy hand and thy counsel determined before to be done.

> And now, Lord, behold their threatenings: and grant unto thy servants, that with all boldness they may speak thy word, by stretching forth thine hand to heal; and that signs and wonders may be done by the name of thy holy child Jesus.

> And when they had prayed, the place was shaken where they were assembled together; and they were all filled with the Holy Ghost, and they spake the word of God with boldness.

> And the multitude of them that believed were of one heart and of one soul.

If you want to know the key to effective united prayer, read that last verse again. **And the multitude of them that believed were of one heart and of one soul.** What makes this kind of prayer work is not how many people you gather. It's the unity of the hearts.

Notice in verse 24, it said they lifted up their voice. Not voices. Not one person lifting up his voice, but all of them lifting up one voice. United prayer is a chorus of people praying with one mind. In heaven, it is recorded as one voice.

Such power can be generated through that kind of unity so that, in this instance, it even shook the building. What's more, this united prayer meeting not only changed circumstances, it changed the people who were praying as well.

Another example of crisis praying is found in Acts 12:1-7.

Now about that time Herod the king stretched forth his hands to vex certain of the church.

And he killed James the brother of John with the sword. And because he saw it pleased the Jews, he proceeded further to take Peter also. (Then were the days of unleavened bread.)

And when he had apprehended him, he put him in prison, and delivered him to four quaternions of soldiers to keep him; intending after Easter to bring him forth to the people.

This certainly constitutes a crisis! Herod had killed James and imprisoned Peter. Fortunately, the Church remembered the power of united prayer before Peter suffered James's fate. Look at what happened when they prayed.

> **Peter therefore was kept in prison: but prayer was made without ceasing of the church unto God for him.**

> **And when Herod would have brought him forth, the same night Peter was sleeping between two soldiers, bound with two chains: and the keepers before the door kept the prison.**

> **And, behold, the angel of the Lord came upon him, and a light shined in the prison: and he smote Peter on the side, and raised him up, saying, Arise up quickly. And his chains fell off from his hands.**

The power of their united prayer stripped off Peter's chains. There are times when the Church needs chain-stripping power today, and united prayer is the way to access it. If you continue reading that chapter, you'll see that an angel appeared in the prison and supernaturally got him out past the soldiers on guard. That's another privilege of united prayer—it brings angels on the scene.

To Obtain Mercy and Forgiveness

The second situation in the Bible where we see united prayer used is when corporate mercy and forgiveness are needed. We find the best example of this kind of prayer in the book of Ezra.

Ezra was a prophet in Israel at a crucial time in the nation's history. Prior to Ezra's day, the children of Israel had gotten mixed up with the heathens and ended up in bondage for seventy years. They were released by Daniel's prayers, and afterwards they went back to Israel to rebuild. Once they arrived, they started intermarrying with heathens again.

When Ezra heard what they'd done, he was so grieved that he tore his garments and his mantle and plucked out his hair and beard. If we knew how much God hates sin, we'd be as sorry as Ezra was. His response to their sin is recorded in Ezra 10:1,2,6-7,9-12.

> Now when Ezra had prayed, and when he had confessed, weeping and casting Himself down before the house of God, there assembled unto him out of Israel a very great congregation of men and women and children: for the people wept very sore.

Ezra wasn't even the one who sinned, but he started the repentance by weeping for the sins of the people. As a result, other people began gathering to weep for their own sins. Finally, the whole congregation of people were repenting.

> And Shechaniah the son of Jehiel, one of the sons of Elam, answered and said unto Ezra, We have trespassed against our God, and have taken strange wives of the people of the land: yet now there is hope in Israel concerning this thing.

> Then Ezra rose up from before the house of God, and went into the chamber of Johanan the son of Eliashib:

and when he came thither, he did eat no bread, nor drink water: for he mourned because of the transgression of them that had been carried away.

And they made proclamation throughout Judah and Jerusalem unto all the children of the captivity, that they should gather themselves together unto Jerusalem; then all the men of Judah and Benjamin gathered themselves together unto Jerusalem within three days. It was the ninth month, on the twentieth day of the month; and all the people sat in the street of the house of God, trembling because of this matter, and for the great rain.

And Ezra the priest stood up, and said unto them, Ye have transgressed, and have taken strange wives, to increase the trespass of Israel. Now therefore make confession unto the Lord God of your fathers, and do his pleasure: and separate yourselves from the people of the land, and from the strange wives.

Then all the congregation answered and said with a loud voice, As thou hast said, so must we do.

What an amazing sight that must have been. The people were so shaken by their sin that they sat in the rain before the presence of God and repented. They used united repentance to keep their nation from coming under a curse, and they received mercy and forgiveness.

A Solemn Assembly

Another example of united prayer calling for mercy and forgiveness is found in the book of Joel. This book is famous for the prophecy that the Lord will pour out His Spirit on all flesh. But have you ever looked back to see what happened before that? It's found in Joel 2:15-17.

> Blow the trumpet in Zion, sanctify a fast, call a solemn assembly: Gather the people, sanctify the congregation, assemble the elders, gather the children, and those that suck the breasts: let the bridegroom go forth of his chamber, and the bride out of her closet.

> Let the priests, the ministers of the Lord, weep between the porch and the altar, and let them say, Spare thy people, O Lord, and give not thine heritage to reproach, that the heathen should rule over them: wherefore should they say among the people, Where is their God?

Actually, in this case, the prophet Joel was warning Israel that because of their sin, a day of judgment was coming. Great calamity was about to hit the nation. The only way to stop it, said the prophet, was for the people to unite in prayer and ask God to forgive and save them.

In both Ezra and Joel's situations, the people praying and seeking God were the children of Israel. But in the book of Jonah we see another story. Jonah 3:5-10 tells of a people who weren't in covenant with God at all. They were outright heathens, yet God sent Jonah to the people of the city of

Nineveh to warn them with a short sermon about the destruction that was coming to their sinful city.

When they heard the Word of the Lord,

> ...the people of Nineveh believed God, and proclaimed a fast, and put on sackcloth, from the greatest of them even to the least of them.

> For word came unto the king of Nineveh, and he arose from his throne, and he laid his robe from him, and covered him with sackcloth, and sat in ashes. And he caused it to be proclaimed and published through Nineveh by the decree of the king and his nobles, saying, let neither man nor beast, herd nor flock, taste any thing: let them not feed, nor drink water: but let man and beast be covered with sackcloth, and cry mightily unto God: yea, let them turn every one from his evil way, and from the violence that is in their hands.

> Who can tell if God will turn and repent, and turn away from his fierce anger, that we perish not?

> And God saw their works, that they turned from their evil way; and God repented of the evil, that he had said that he would do unto them; and he did it not.

This whole town fasted and prayed together before God. Their children didn't eat or drink. They wouldn't even let their dogs or cats drink. Instead, they repented, and it stopped the judgment.

Unified Worship

❧

Worship is the most common way that believers come together in unity before God. People in churches all over the world worship together every Sunday. Even so, we rarely see the powerful results we should because, in most cases, the voices of the people are in harmony, but their hearts are not. For the power of God to be manifested, those gathered must be in one accord.

In 2 Chronicles 5:11-14 NKJV, we see that when Israel came together for the dedication of Solomon's temple, they lifted up their voices in one accord, and the glory cloud rolled into the house.

> And it came to pass when the priests came out of the Most Holy Place (for all the priests who were present had sanctified themselves, without keeping to their divisions), and the Levites who were the singers, all those of Asaph and Heman and Jeduthun, with their sons and their brethren, stood at the east end of the altar, clothed in white linen, having cymbals, stringed instruments and harps, and with them one hundred and twenty priests sounding with trumpets—indeed it came to pass, when the trumpeters and singers were as one, to make one sound to be heard in praising and thanking the Lord, and when they lifted up their voice with the trumpets and cymbals and instruments of music, and praised the Lord, saying: "For He is good, for His mercy endures forever," that the house, the house of the Lord, was filled with a

IN ONE
ACCORD

cloud, so that the priests could not continue ministering because of the cloud; for the glory of the Lord filled the house of God.

This is the very reason that it is so important that the music ministry be in one accord, as well as those gathered corporately. Great power is available when God's people worship in real unity.

According to 1 Timothy 3:15, there is a way to behave in the house of God. **But if I tarry long, that thou mayest know how thou oughtest to behave thyself in the house of God, which is the church of the living God, the pillar and ground of the truth.**

How were the people behaving when the glory cloud rolled in? They were worshipping and praising God in one accord. That's how we're to behave in the house of God. You won't see the manifest presence of God if part of the people are praising in one accord and others are thinking about the roast they have at home in the oven. *AGREEMENT IS KEY!*

Another example of unified worship is found in Acts 16:25: **And at midnight Paul and Silas prayed, and sang praises unto God: and the prisoners heard them.** Here, we find Paul and Silas in a critical situation. They'd been beaten and imprisoned. It was truly a midnight hour for them. Certainly they needed to pray. But I want you to notice that they didn't stop at prayer. The Bible says that they prayed *and* sang praises. Often people will pray, and pray, and pray and pray. But Paul and Silas prayed and sang praises.

Do you know what happened as they praised God together in that jail? God sent an earthquake! It shook all the doors open, and everyone's bands were loosed. Their feet were in stocks, but the earthquake set them free.

There are times when we need nothing more than to pray and praise, because that's the combination that will bring down the power of God and set us free.

Seeking Direction

The fourth kind of situation that calls for unified prayer is one where a group of people need guidance from God. We find the Jews facing such a situation in 2 Chronicles 20:13-18. There we see the whole country of Judah in trouble. They were about to be attacked by three different armies at the same time, and they didn't know what to do. Should they run, surrender or fight? No one but God Himself could tell them, so they gathered to seek direction from the Lord. **And all Judah stood before the Lord, with their little ones, their wives, and their children** (v. 13).

They brought their wives, children and babies. The youth came. The old people came. Everyone gathered to seek God. They didn't leave it up to the leaders. Look what happened.

Then upon Jahaziel the son Zechariah, the son of Benaiah, the son of Jeiel, the son of Mattaniah, a Levite of the sons of Asaph, came the Spirit of the Lord in the midst of the congregation; and he said, Hearken ye, all

Judah, and ye inhabitants of Jerusalem, and thou king Jehoshaphat, Thus saith the Lord unto you, Be not afraid nor dismayed by reason of this great multitude; for the battle is not yours, but God's.

Tomorrow go ye down against them: behold, they come up by the cliff of Ziz; and ye shall find them at the end of the brook, before the wilderness of Jeruel. Ye shall not need to fight in this battle: set yourselves, stand ye still, and see the salvation of the Lord with you, O Judah and Jerusalem: fear not, nor be dismayed; tomorrow go out against them: for the Lord will be with you.

And Jehoshaphat bowed his head with his face to the ground: and all Judah and the inhabitants of Jerusalem fell before the Lord, worshipping the Lord.

When everyone sought the Lord, He spoke to them through a prophet and declared, "Stand still and see the salvation of the Lord. The battle is not yours, but God's!"

The people of Judah believed that prophecy and obeyed the instructions God gave them in it. They went out against the enemy the next day, singing and praising God. They didn't have to fight at all. God sent an angelic ambush, defeated the opposing armies supernaturally, and God's people simply picked up the spoil for three days. This kind of victory would not have happened if the king had gone alone into his prayer closet to pray. It required the power of unified prayer.

As we learn to gather in unity to pray, we, too, will see more amazing victories in our churches and in our nation. We will discover just as these did that when a group of people join together to seek God, He will be found.

5

❧

The Prayer of Praise, Worship and Thanksgiving

Through Him therefore let us constantly and at all times offer up to God a sacrifice of praise, which is the fruit of lips that thankfully acknowledge and confess and glorify His name.

Hebrews 13:15 AMP

We pray for many reasons. At times we pray to receive wisdom and guidance. Other times, we pray just because we want to fellowship with God. But the truth is that a great majority of the time, we pray because we need the power of God to work on our behalf.

In the past, traditional religious teachings have often discouraged us from trying to learn too much about how to understand and tap into that power. They promoted the idea that God intends for His power to remain a mysteriously unpredictable force that strikes like lightning wherever and whenever you least expect it.

But the Bible doesn't say any such thing. In the prayers of the apostle Paul, he tells us that it's God's will for us to **know and understand what is the immeasurable and unlimited and surpassing greatness of His power in and for us who believe** (Eph. 1:18 AMP).

Clearly, God's power is not meant to remain a mystery to us. He wants us to know how it works and how it flows. He wants us to understand how He moves and how to move with Him. Of course, it would be impossible to do a thorough study on the power of God in this one book. But we can look at a few Scriptures to see what kinds of things we can expect from it.

First of all, John 1:1-5 says,

In the beginning was the Word, and the Word was with God, and the Word was God. The same was in the beginning with God.

All things were made by him; and without him was not any thing made that was made.

In him was life; and the life was the light of men. And the light shineth in darkness; and the darkness comprehended it not.

We see there that the power of God is identified as life, light and the ability to create. Therefore, if you have sickness in your body, you can expect the life of God to drive it out. If you have darkness and oppression, the light of God will free you. If you are lacking something good, the God who made all things can create it for you.

Acts 10:38 confirms those operations of the power of God. It says that **God anointed Jesus of Nazareth with the Holy Ghost and with power: who went about doing good, and healing all that were oppressed of the Devil; for God was with him.**

In Romans 6:4, we see that Jesus was raised from the dead by the glory (or power) of God. **Therefore we are buried with him by baptism into death: that like as Christ was raised up from the dead by the glory of the Father, even so we also should walk in newness of life.** When your hopes and dreams are as good as dead, when you are past human help, the power of God can raise you up.

Plug Into the Power

What kinds of prayer best access that power?

Actually, every prayer prayed in faith will to some degree bring the power of God on the scene. But there is one prayer that is particularly effective, and it is often overlooked—not only in our daily lives, but also in times of need and crisis, when we require God's power the most.

It is the prayer of praise, worship and thanksgiving.

In chapter 4, we saw that so much of the power of God was released when the Israelites worshipped God in one accord at the dedication of Solomon's temple that it knocked down all the ministers. The Bible says that the house of the Lord was filled with a cloud so that the priests could not continue to minister, because the glory of God filled the temple.

Obviously, in Solomon's day, worship was not just the time during the Sunday service when music was sung and latecomers were seated. It wasn't just a convenient element used to bring two parts of the service together. It was a time when the people truly bowed their hearts and worshipped God.

Many believers today don't know much about that kind of heartfelt worship. Instead they've become experts at saying, "Praise God. Praise God," with their mouths while their minds and hearts are focused on something else altogether. We've all done that at times, and when we do, we are not plugging into the power of God.

We might be saying, "Hallelujah, Lord!" on the outside, but on the inside we're thinking about how badly our children have been acting lately or how we're going to pay the phone bill. We might be singing praises to God while wondering where the pastor's wife bought the dress she's wearing. I'm sure you know as well as I do, that kind of worship isn't going to flood the church with the power of God.

It Makes a Difference

Some people might think it's no big deal when they let their minds wander during worship. They might think it doesn't make any difference whether they spend any time at home just praising, worshipping and thanking God. But, the fact is, it makes a big difference.

A few years ago, God spoke to me specifically about that. I'll never forget the day. I'd gotten some bad news that had really hit me hard. Instead of crying out in tears to God, I fell down on my face and began worshipping Him. I praised Him for His love and protection. I honored Him.

After a while, the Spirit of the Lord said, *Get your Bible. I want to show you why My people are not receiving the fulfillment of My promises. I want you to see why they aren't receiving health and healing; why they aren't receiving prosperity and riches.*

The verse God took me to was Psalm 112:1 AMP: **Praise the Lord!—Hallelujah! Blessed—happy, fortunate [to be envied]—is the man who fears [reveres and worships] the Lord, who delights greatly in His commandments.**

The rest of the psalm goes on to list the blessings we all want. It says the person who worships God will have mighty offspring. Wealth and riches will be in his house. He'll have light during dark times and victory over every enemy.

Do you want that kind of life? Do you want your children to be mighty? Do you want to prosper? Then worship God.

Praise Him unashamedly. If you're having financial problems, it could be because you're not worshipping God in your house. If you make worship a lifestyle in your home, God will visit you with an abundance of blessings.

Why is it so important to worship? First of all, because God is God and He deserves to be worshipped. He gave us every good thing we have and not to worship Him is a sin. It's arrogant and ungrateful to take what He gives and not bless Him in return.

The second reason it's important to worship is that God has ordained it as a way for us to access His power. Worship releases His blessings on our behalf.

I had some kind of stomach virus one day and was very sick, so I began confessing Exodus 23:25. I said, "Lord, You bless my bread. You bless my water. You take sickness from the midst of me." I repeated those words over and over.

Finally, the Lord said, "No!" So, I opened my Bible, and He made me back up and read the first part of that verse. It said, **You shall worship the Lord your God, and I will bless your bread and your water; and I will take sickness away from among you** (NRSV). I quickly realized that if I worshipped God right then and there, then worship would open the way for me to receive the healing power of God.

One reason worship paves the way for God to move is because worship is the language of faith. If you believe that God heard you pray and that He's moving on your behalf, you'll thank Him.

How Much Is Too Much?

Someone might say, "Well, I just believe you're getting carried away with this praise and worship business. After all, God doesn't expect us to be doing that all the time."

Yes, actually He does.

Hebrews 13:15 AMP says, **Through Him therefore let us constantly and at all times offer up to God a sacrifice of praise, which is the fruit of lips that thankfully acknowledge and confess and glorify His name.** Psalms 34:1 AMP says, **I will bless the Lord at all times; His praise shall continually be in my mouth.**

Such a lifestyle of worship isn't just for mature, seasoned saints, either. Luke 24 tells how Jesus visited the early Church after He'd been raised from the dead. These people were just a few days old in the Lord; yet the Bible says,

> **And he led them out as far as to Bethany, and he lifted up his hands, and blessed them. And it came to pass, while he blessed them, he was parted from them, and carried up into heaven.**
>
> **And they worshipped him, and returned to Jerusalem with great joy: and were continually in the temple, praising and blessing God.**
>
> LUKE 24:50-53

Praise should be the language of people who believe that God is on the throne, and that Jesus is at His right hand. It is the language of those who know that He sent the Comforter. It is for those who understand that Jesus "ever lives to make intercession for us." We have much to be thankful for, and we should continually be praising God in our earthly temple. We see a scriptural picture of this thankfulness in Acts 2.

> And they, continuing daily with one accord in the temple, and breaking bread from house to house, did eat their meat with gladness and singleness of heart, praising God, and having favour with all the people. And the Lord added to the church daily such as should be saved.
>
> ACTS 2:46,47

Paul's Prayers

Philippians 4:6 AMP tells us, **Do not fret or have any anxiety about anything, but in every circumstance and in everything by prayer and petition [definite requests] with thanksgiving continue to make your wants known to God.** Why does it say "with thanksgiving"? As I said before, it's because if you believe God heard your prayer and supplication, you'll be thankful.

You can tell which people are doing business with God on a regular basis because they're always praising Him. They always have something going with God to thank Him for. If there isn't a lot of praise in your life, step up your prayer life, and you'll have more reason to be thankful.

I believe that God is just waiting for us to ask something. He wants to hear from us all the time, and I want to keep Him busy. When He finds someone who'll pray, He'll give them something to praise Him for.

Paul not only gave us instruction about giving thanks, he gave us his own example as well. He must have been one of the most praying and praising men who ever walked on earth. We find examples of this throughout the New Testament. According to 1 Corinthians 1:4, which states, **I thank my God always on your behalf, for the grace of God which is given you by Jesus Christ,** Paul was always thanking God.

In Ephesians 1:16, Paul says, **[I] cease not to give thanks for you, making mention of you in my prayers.** He wasn't praying just for the church at Ephesus; he was constantly giving thanks. We need to do the same thing. When you think of a body of believers, a pastor, or your friend, thank your heavenly Father for them.

In Philippians 1:3-4, Paul added, **I thank my God upon every remembrance of you, always in every prayer of mine for you all making request with joy.**

One of the pitfalls praying people fall into is that they become heavy with the burdens of prayer, and it gets coupled with spiritual pride. "I'm a pray-er, and I'm just weighted down with it so heavily today!" Well, you shouldn't be. You're not God, and you aren't carrying the world on your shoulders. You're just doing your part in prayer.

So what keeps the heaviness away? Worshipping God with praise and thanksgiving. It will keep you focused on God instead of on yourself. It will keep your prayers clean, and it will protect you from taking either the credit or the responsibility for doing God's part.

In Colossians 1:3, Paul said, **We give thanks to God and the Father of our Lord Jesus Christ, praying always for you.** Don't you love Paul? This man had to be continually praying! He communed with God all the time. I like what a great preacher once said, "I never pray for more than fifteen minutes, but I never go more than fifteen minutes without praying."[1] Like this preacher, if we believe God is with us all the time, then we'll be conferring with Him continually.

In 1 Thessalonians 1:2, Paul said, **We give thanks to God always for you all, making mention of you in our prayers.** We need to follow Paul's example and make mention of people's names when we pray. If someone comes to your mind, lift them up to the throne of grace. "Father, I lift up...." Make mention of them in your prayers.

In 1 Thessalonians 2:13, Paul said, **For this cause also thank we God without ceasing.** Paul was extreme in the very best sense of the word when you compare his prayer life with that of most Christians. He prayed without ceasing.

In 2 Thessalonians 1:3, Paul wrote, **We are bound to thank God always for you, brethren, as it is meet, because that your faith groweth exceedingly, and the charity of every one of you all toward each other aboundeth.**

There will always be evidence of what the Devil is trying to do in someone's life, but don't focus on that. Magnify what God's doing. "Isn't it terrible what's happening to So-and-So?" someone might say. Don't get into that. Sniff at the Devil and talk about what God is doing about the situation. If you don't see evidence of it in their lives, go to the Bible. Remember that if they're born again, you have God's Word that He is working in them, both to will and to do His good pleasure. (Phil. 3:13.) Grab hold of that and magnify it. Boast in the Lord! Even if you have to look at the situation under a magnifying glass, find something in it to thank God for and then open your mouth and let the praises fly.

In the Midnight Hour

Earlier in our study of united prayer, we looked at two scriptural examples of believers who prayed together in times of crisis and tapped into the mighty power of God. I want to look at those examples again here, because the kind of prayer those believers were praying was the prayer of worship and thanksgiving. And though in those instances there were two or more praying together, this kind of prayer can work for us as individuals too.

In Acts, we saw Paul and Silas in trouble during one of their missionary journeys. Their preaching had made some people mad.

And the multitude rose up together against them: and the magistrates rent off their clothes, and commanded to beat them.

And when they had laid many stripes upon them, they cast them into prison, charging the jailor to keep them safely: Who, having received such a charge, thrust them into the inner prison, and made their feet fast in the stocks.

And at midnight Paul and Silas prayed, and sang praises unto God: and the prisoners heard them.

Acts 16:22-25

We've all encountered our midnight hour—both by the clock and by the crisis. It's the darkest time. What do you do when you find yourself in a crisis at midnight? Do exactly what Paul and Silas did. They prayed and sang praises unto God. You can't afford to wait until you feel like praising God. If Paul and Silas had waited until they felt like praising God, they would never have tapped into the power they needed to get them through the crisis.

But, thank God, they did tap into that power and it literally shook the prison. **Immediately all the doors were opened, and every one's bands were loosed** (v. 26). By the time the night was over, Paul and Silas were free, the jailer and his whole family had been saved and they were all rejoicing together over dinner. Now that's what I call victory!

Kenneth E. Hagin's book, *Prevailing Prayer to Peace,* gives a modern-day example of some believers he knew who discovered how praise could bring the power of God at the midnight hour. They were called to pray for a child who was in the throes of terrible convulsions. They prayed, bound and rebuked, but nothing happened. The child simply wouldn't stop convulsing. Finally, they were exhausted from praying, and the pastor's wife began singing praises to the Lord very quietly. Suddenly, everyone just stopped thinking about the child and started thinking about the Lord and praising Him. When they did, the child quit convulsing. Why? Because praise released their faith!

When they relaxed and began to fellowship among themselves, the child began convulsing again. So they started praying real hard—binding, loosing, rebuking and casting out. I'm not saying those were wrong prayers, but their faith wasn't released until, once more, they began singing praises to God. Again, the convulsions stopped.[1]

Their experience proved what the Bible says to be so. There is power in praise that cannot be accessed any other way.

Take Every Thought Captive

There's another reason the prayer of worship and praise is a good prayer to pray during times of crisis. It keeps your mind at peace. It keeps you focused on what God will do for you instead of on what the Devil is trying to do to you.

Remember the Old Testament account of Jehoshaphat we studied earlier? No doubt when the people of Judah found out that three enemy armies were coming against them, their minds were troubled. They were assaulted by fears and thoughts of what could happen to them and their children in such a battle.

When they united in prayer and asked God for help, **He said, Hearken ye, all Judah, and ye inhabitants of Jerusalem, and thou king Jehoshaphat, Thus saith the Lord unto you, Be not afraid nor dismayed by reason of this great multitude; for the battle is not yours, but God's** (2 Chron. 20:15).

What a relief it must have been for the children of Israel to hear God say that He would fight their battle. But that's not all He told them. He also told them not to be afraid. When God says not to be afraid, it is in bad taste and bad manners to be afraid.

How did they respond to that command? With a powerful demonstration of thanksgiving.

> **Ye shall not need to fight in this battle: set yourselves, stand ye still, and see the salvation of the Lord with you, O Judah and Jerusalem: fear not, nor be dismayed; tomorrow go out against them: for the Lord will be with you.**
>
> **And Jehoshaphat bowed his head with his face to the ground: and all Judah and the inhabitants of Jerusalem fell before the Lord, worshipping the Lord.**
>
> **And the Levites, of the children of the Kohathites, and of the children of the Korhites, stood up to praise the Lord God of Israel with a loud voice on high.**
>
> 2 CHRONICLES 20:17-19

They didn't stop praising God after that service was over either. The next day when the Judaean army went out to fight,

King Jehoshaphat **appointed singers unto the Lord, and that should praise the beauty of holiness, as they went out before the army, and to say, Praise the Lord; for his mercy endureth for ever. And when they began to sing and to praise, the Lord set ambushments...and they [their enemies] were smitten** (v. 21,22).

I don't believe that Jehoshaphat put those praisers out front just because he thought that would be cute. I believe he was led by the Holy Spirit to do it because He knew those praises would keep the people from falling prey to thoughts of fear when they were marching out to meet the enemy armies.

When you've prayed about a crisis and received a word from the Lord, the Holy Spirit will lead you to do the same thing. And you'd better do it. If you don't control your thoughts, the Devil will drive you crazy with worry. Thoughts can be so heinous. They're like a little television inside your brain. You're always seeing pictures of something in there. And if you aren't running pictures of praise—pictures of what God has promised to do for you, pictures of past victories He has given you—the Devil will surely make you watch some programs he put together. Then you'll lose your faith and slip into fear.

Remembering

Notice I said that when you need to praise in times of crisis, you can not only praise God for what He's promised to do for you in this situation, you can praise Him for what He has done for you in past situations. Time and again in the Bible, God admonishes His people to remember what He has done for them.

David said, **I will [earnestly] recall the deeds of the Lord; yes, I will [earnestly] remember the wonders [You performed for our fathers] of old. I will meditate also upon all Your work and consider all Your [mighty] deeds** (Ps. 77:11,12 AMP).

One of the key ingredients in true worship is remembering. What do you need to remember? All the marvelous things God has done for you in the past. You remember all the marvelous promises He gave us in the Bible. You remember what He has done for others. You call those things to account by acknowledging them with your mouth. Each time you do it, it rekindles your faith.

In Judges 5, before the people of God went out to battle, they rehearsed the righteous acts of God. They took turns standing and remembering what God had done for them in the past.

Deuteronomy 7:17-18 gives us a stern warning. There the Lord told the Israelites not to say in their hearts, **These nations are more than I; how can I dispossess them? Thou shalt not be afraid of them.** In other words, don't say in your heart, "This disease is too bad. How can God heal me?" "This problem is bigger than I am." "These bills are insurmountable." "I can't get over this hurt."

God commands us not to be afraid of those things.

So what should we do?

Remember.

Thou shalt not be afraid of them: but shalt well remember what the Lord thy God did unto Pharaoh, and unto all Egypt; the great temptations which thine eyes saw, and the signs, and the wonders, and the mighty hand, and the stretched out arm, whereby the Lord thy God brought thee out: so shall the Lord thy God do unto all the people of whom thou art afraid.

DEUTERONOMY 7:18,19

Remembering will work against fear. Have you ever found yourself in the midst of a difficult situation, thinking, *What am I going to do?* The next time that happens, stop and remember the times God has delivered you from the enemy's trap. Remember the times God delivered others. And remember—if He has done it before, He can do it again.

Don't Forget

Psalm 103:2 tells us, **Bless the Lord, O my soul, and forget not all his benefits.** The key words here are *forget not.* That means it is possible to forget. Maybe you've already forgotten what God has done for you. That's okay. Ask Him to forgive you and purposely start to remember all these things. You can remember what God did in the Bible. What Jesus did to the Devil. What God has done for other people. You need to keep a catalog of all God's credentials, because He has never failed.

There is an old hymn that tells us to count our blessings and name them one by one. When you count your blessings, it takes your focus off what the Devil is doing, and it hooks you into the power of God.

Beliefs are based on evidence, so the Devil will always try to give you contrary evidence. Praise will help you stay assured of what you believe. And worship holds your place in faith. If you begin to totter, praise God. Never forget that the Bible says you have a way of escape. It doesn't matter how far down you are, God has a way to lift you up and out. He has a *high way* for you—and it is paved with praise.

6

The Prayer of Faith

*And Jesus answering saith unto them, Have faith
in God. For verily I say unto you, That whosoever
shall say unto this mountain, Be thou removed,
and be thou cast into the sea; and shall not doubt
in his heart, but shall believe that those things
which he saith shall come to pass; he shall have
whatsoever he saith. Therefore I say unto you,
What things soever ye desire, when ye pray, believe
that ye receive them, and ye shall have them.*

MARK 11:22-24

Every prayer we pray requires faith in order to be effective.
I often think of faith as the vehicle you ride in when you
pray. The more faith you have, the faster you can move
toward your answer. You can travel either by pony express or
by Concorde. It all depends on the level of your faith.

If you are praying the prayer of consecration, for example, surrendering yourself to the will of God, you must believe that God hears your prayer and responds to it. You may not know specifically what the will of God is for you at that moment. But you must trust that He will receive your surrender and guide you into the knowledge of that will.

Likewise, in the prayer of praise and worship or the prayer of casting your care, you must release faith, believing that God hears and receives your prayers.

The prayer we call the prayer of faith, however, requires a different kind of believing. It requires us not just to trust that God hears and receives our prayer, but that He will respond in a specific way. To pray the prayer of faith, we must know without a doubt what the will of God is about the particular thing we are addressing in prayer. We must be so certain He will give it to us that we can ask once, thank Him for His answer and—regardless of what we see or feel—believe with certainty that He has granted our request.

If you study Jesus' teaching about this kind of prayer in Mark 11:22-24, you'll see there are two parts to it. There is a *praying* part and a *saying* part. Often, people will read verse 23 about speaking to the mountain and they'll want to jump right into the saying part. Without any spiritual preparation, they'll start speaking to situations in their lives, ordering them to be removed or changed. When their words don't seem to have the intended effect, they get discouraged and give up on the prayer of faith altogether.

What they don't realize is they should have done some preparation first. They should have spent some time fellow-shipping with the Lord about their situation. They should have read the Word, sought the will of the Lord and communed with the Holy Spirit until they'd received clear direction from Him about how to pray and what to say. I like to say it this way: sometimes you have to pray some other kinds of prayer before you can effectively pray the prayer of faith. You have to pray before you pray and pray before you say. So let's study verse 24 which speaks about praying first.

What Things Soever Ye Desire, When Ye Pray

The first word I want you to notice here is the simple word *pray*. If you'll study the implications of that word, you'll find that in its most simple form, prayer is a communication directed toward God.

I know that sounds so simple it hardly seems worth mentioning but, actually, it's a vital principle. If you want to be effective in prayer, you must remember as you pray that you are speaking *to God*.

This is so important that I'm going to say it again. One of the greatest keys to success in prayer is being consciously aware that you are speaking to God when you pray!

Maybe you're so spiritual this has never happened to you, but many times I've found myself praying along, just shooting out my requests as hard and fast as I could, and I suddenly realized I had absolutely <u>no consciousness of God</u>. I wasn't <u>thinking about Him</u>. I wasn't really talking to Him. <u>My mind</u> <u>was totally focused on what I needed and what I wanted</u>. I was just throwing religious cliches into the air, hoping it would do some good.

At other times, I've found my <u>mind wandering</u> while I was trying to pray. I'd be saying words to God with my mouth, but my mind and my heart were off somewhere else. As a result, my prayers were weak and ineffective.

Communicated w/ God

Actually, God isn't the only one I've treated that way. I've done the same thing to my husband. At those times, I'd be trying to talk to him while doing several other things at the same time. I'd get a few words out, and my mind would wander. I wouldn't even finish a sentence before I'd be off on another topic. My communication would be so scattered, my husband could hardly understand what I was saying.

Do you know what my husband does when I act like that? He sits me down in front of him and makes me look at him while I talk. He makes me focus not just on what I'm saying but on the fact that I am saying it *to him!*

Know what you are say and know who you are saying it to!

I've found the same tactic works when I am talking to God. If I will take the time to focus my attention directly on Him, if I will make myself become conscious that I am coming before His throne and He is listening to me, it will change the way I pray.

1. Focus on God
2. Be conscious you are coming to the

It's a simple truth, but if you'll put it to work in your prayer life, you'll find it has a powerful effect.

The second word I want you to take notice of in this first part of verse 24 is the word *desire*. If you were to investigate the full meaning of that word in the Greek, you'd find it means more than just wanting something. It means expressing that desire by making a request.[1] Several more modern versions of the New Testament use the word *ask* there instead of the word *desire*.

So, you could more literally translate verse 24 to read this way: **What things soever ye desire** [enough to ask], **when ye pray....**

Once again, this may sound like a very simple truth, but it is important so I'm going to say it. When the Bible says *ask*, it means *ask*. Asking isn't commanding. Asking isn't saying, "I receive." Asking isn't thanking. Asking is asking!

Some people seem to want to skip over the asking part. They've heard somebody else pray and thank God for something, so they'll imitate that prayer and just say, "Father, I thank You that I have the money for the new car I want." There is a place for that kind of prayer, and we'll discuss that a little later. But for now, let's get the progression straight.

Asking is where we begin. We go to the throne of God and ask as a child would ask of a father. We say something like, "Father God, I need this, and Your Word says You have provided for me, so I am asking You for it. I believe I receive it now. Thank You."

Notice in that little prayer, our request was not addressed to Jesus. Sometimes I'll hear new believers who don't know much about the Word asking Jesus for things. No doubt, God makes allowances for their immaturity, but it's important for us to grow up and do things the way He tells us to. And Jesus very clearly instructed us how we are to address our requests.

He said in John 16:23,26-27, **Verily, verily, I say unto you, Whatsoever ye shall ask the Father in my name, he will give it you. At that day ye shall ask in my name: and I say not unto you, that I will pray the Father for you: for the Father Himself loveth you, because ye have loved me, and have believed that I came out from God.**

In essence, Jesus was saying, "Don't ask Me to ask the Father for you. Don't turn your prayer life over to Me. You're a son of God now. You ask the Father yourself. You have just as much of a right to ask Him for things as I do." Isn't that amazing? We all have great confidence in Jesus' prayers. But, the fact is, we should have just as much confidence in our own!

Please understand, I'm not saying that you can't talk to Jesus. You can talk to Him and fellowship with Him all you want. But when it comes time for you to ask God to move on a situation or meet a need, you should speak directly to the Father.

James 1:17 says, **Every good gift and every perfect gift is from above, and cometh down from the Father of lights, with whom is no variableness, neither shadow of turning.** The power and provision you need is going to come from the Father Himself so you need to direct your requests to Him.

Of course, you don't come on your own merit, you come in Jesus' name. That doesn't mean you just say the phrase "in Jesus' name" like a cliché every time you pray. Praying in Jesus' name means praying His will and His desire. It means praying what He would pray if He were in your situation.

That's why in John 15:7, Jesus said, **If ye abide in me, and my words abide in you, ye shall ask what ye will, and it shall be done unto you.** When you're abiding in Jesus, obeying His commands and acting on His Words, you have confidence when you come before the Father. You know He'll hear and answer you just as quickly as He'd hear and answer Jesus Himself because you're acting as Jesus' ambassador here on the earth. You are really, truly praying in His name.

Why Is Asking So Important?

In Matthew 7:7-11, Jesus taught some more about asking.

Ask, and it shall be given you; seek, and ye shall find; knock, and it shall be opened unto you: For every one that asketh receiveth; and he that seeketh findeth; and to him that knocketh it shall be opened.

Or what man is there of you, whom if his son ask bread, will he give him a stone? Or if he ask a fish, will he give him a serpent?

If ye then, being evil, know how to give good gifts unto your children, how much more shall your Father which is in heaven give good things to them that ask him?

In those three verses alone, Jesus refers to asking five times. Clearly, asking is a vital part of receiving from God. Yet in Matthew 6:8, Jesus says, **Your Father knoweth what things ye have need of, before ye ask him.**

If God already knows what we need, why do we have to ask Him for it? Why doesn't He just give it to us?

The answer is simple. Our faith is what connects us to God. It opens the door for us to receive His provision. And asking is an expression of faith.

James 4:2 says, **Ye have not, because ye ask not.** Over the years as I've worked in ministry, I've known of people who wrote and asked for agreement in prayer, and they received the answer to that prayer even before their letter reached us. Many times, we don't even have to pray and agree with people because their prayer has already been answered by the time we receive their letter.

Why is that? It's because when they wrote down their request, they released their faith, and God immediately moved on it!

Faith moves the hand of God in your life. As soon as God gets your faith, He moves His hand and does what you need Him to do.

All we have to do is ask Him in faith.

Know What You Believe

Before you can ask God for something in faith, however, you must know what He has said about it. You must know whether it's His will for you to have it. If you think about it, that makes perfect sense. It's true in any relationship.

Say, for example, you wanted to ask me to buy you a new pair of shoes. You couldn't ask me in faith because I haven't said anything to you about that. You could ask me if it was my will or my desire to buy you a pair of shoes. But you couldn't ask me with confident expectation that I would do it because I might say, no.

If, however, you knew me to be a person of my word and I had said last week that I would buy you a pair of shoes, you could ask me in faith. You could come to me boldly, remind me of my promise and ask me to fulfill it. You could say, "You promised me a new pair of shoes last week. And right now I need that pair of shoes. So would you please buy them for me? Thank you!"

You wouldn't have to worry and wonder if I wanted to buy the shoes. You'd know I want to buy them because I already told you so. You wouldn't have to wonder if I had the money, either. You'd know that, as a person of integrity, I wouldn't have promised to buy the shoes if I didn't have the resources to do so. Because you already knew my will and my ability in the matter, you could ask in faith believing you would receive what you asked.

The prayer of faith works exactly that same way. Before you can pray it, you must settle two questions. First, you must know God's ability. You must be certain He is able to do what you are about to ask Him.

"That's easy," you might say. "God is able to do anything." Actually, that's not totally true. Although God's power is unlimited, He has limited Himself by His own Word. For example, He has said in His Word that whosoever calls on the name of the Lord will be saved. Therefore, if you ask God to save someone, despite the fact that they refuse to call on Him for salvation, He will have to deny your request. He is unable to do that because it would violate the principles He has already established.

Psalm 138:2 says God has magnified His Word above His name. So before you can pray the prayer of faith, you must go to the Bible and make sure God is able to answer that prayer without violating His Word.

The second question you must settle before you pray this prayer is the question of God's will. You must know not only that God is able to do what you ask but that He is willing to do it in this particular case. So, again, you must go to His Word and see what He has said.

Knowing the Word of God is vital to the prayer of faith. That's why Jesus said, **If ye abide in me, and my words abide in you, ye shall ask what ye will, and it shall be done unto you** (Jn. 15:7).

So before you pray the prayer of faith, get out your Bible. Find promises that pertain to what you need. Read them and meditate on them until you know that you believe them. Get them so settled in your heart that you are fully assured you will receive the fulfillment of those promises when you pray.

Notice I said you need to be fully assured *when* you pray, not afterwards. Matthew 21:22 confirms that statement. There Jesus said, **All things, whatsoever ye shall ask in prayer, believing, ye shall receive.**

Sometimes we ask God for things too quickly. We think, *Oh, I know what the Bible says about that!* And without so much as looking up one Scripture, we jump up and start petitioning God for things. Then later we realize we had questions. We start wondering if God is really going to do what we asked, and we realize we weren't in faith.

At that point, we'll usually try to build ourselves up into faith by straining ourselves and saying, "I believe…I believe…I believe." But it doesn't work because it's not the scriptural way.

Whenever I think of this kind of preparation, I'm reminded of the days when I used to travel with a ministry team. I spent many hours in truck stops as we drove from one city to another, and I began to watch the truck drivers. One thing they did was test the wheels on their trucks. If they'd spent the night at the truck stop and their big 18-wheeler had been sitting in one spot for hours, before they took it back on the highway, they'd get a long pole and walk around the truck banging on the wheels. They'd hit one wheel, and that pole would make a sound. *Boing!* Then they'd hit the next one. *Boing!*

I learned that what they were doing was checking the tire pressure. They'd hit each wheel with that pole and listen to the tone it made, and that would tell them whether the tires had the proper amount of air. They didn't want to find out one of those tires was low *after* they'd gotten the truck rolling and they were already moving down the highway. They wanted to find out *before* they got started.

That's the way it is with the prayer of faith. You don't want to find out you aren't in faith after your prayer is already rolling. You want to hit those faith wheels before you begin. Listen to the tone of your heart on the matter, and if you aren't fully confident you'll receive what you ask when you pray, air up your spiritual tires. Spend some time building them up with the promises of God.

That's not to say you can't pray at all until you're established in faith about that particular matter. You can pray a great deal during the time you are getting established. You can say, "Father, I'm not fully confident of Your will and Your ability in this matter. Please help me find some Scriptures that will help me. Show me what Your Word says about this area of my life. Illuminate my heart where this is concerned."

But you don't want to make your request, you don't want to present your formal petition, until you are established in your faith.

This is so important that many times when I pray this kind of prayer, I'll write down the date and the time that I prayed. I'll write down the Scriptures that I based my faith on. I'll put it in black and white so I'll know that it's settled. I'll know that on this day at this time I asked God for a certain thing, and I believed I received. Therefore, it is mine!

That way, I'll be ready when the Devil comes with contrary evidence and tries to shake my faith. When he comes and says, "Well, nothing happened when you prayed because you don't feel any different. Your circumstances don't look any different," I won't waver.

James 1:6-7 says, **He that wavereth is like a wave of the sea driven with the wind and tossed. For let not that man think that he shall receive any thing of the Lord.** The wavering person who hasn't built a foundation of faith on the Word of God will change with every day that goes by. If something good happens in that circumstance he prayed about, he'll be happy. He'll say, "Hallelujah! God is answering my prayer." The next day, when something bad happens, he'll say, "Oh my, I guess God didn't answer me after all." God can't do anything for a person like that because he hasn't established his faith connection.

When you take the time to get firmly established in your faith, you won't be moved by what the situation looks like. You won't be moved by how you feel on any given day, because you're not basing your confidence on what you see and what you feel; you're basing it on the unchangeable Word of God!

First John 5:14-15 says, **This is the confidence that we have in him, that, if we ask any thing according to his will, he heareth us: and if we know that he hear us, whatsoever we ask, we know that we have the petitions that we desired of him.**

That's strong language. It says when we know we are asking God for something that He wills to give us, we *know*—we don't just hope, we don't just think, we *know*—we have what we asked!

I've experienced that kind of knowing myself. There are times when I so prepared myself to present my petition to God that I was overflowing with confidence by the time I got to His throne. I was so certain of what His Word said, I was so sure of His will, that I knew without a shadow of a doubt that the moment I spoke that request, the answer was mine.

Granted, it takes a little time to get yourself to that place of faith, but it's time well spent. If you're tempted to skip it, remember this—once you've prayed, the Devil will come and try to steal your faith. He always does. He will try to rob you of what you believe because he knows that all things are possible to those who believe.

So he'll try to make you look like a fool for believing God. He'll set up circumstances to make your faith look like a farce. He'll use physical evidence to undermine your confidence in God's Word. He'll do everything he can to make it look like that word is untrue. He started doing that in the second chapter of Genesis, and he hasn't stopped since.

Actually, most of what the Devil does is simply designed to make you change what you believe. It's not designed to kill you. That isn't the best way he can get at God. The best way he can get at God is to convince you to look in God's face and say, "Your Word is not true."

If the Devil can do that, he has scored. He's backed you into a corner and neutralized you so that you can't do anything to hurt him. And he's insulted God by getting one of His own children to call Him a liar.

So take the time to get firmly settled on the Word. Get in the place of faith and then refuse to move. Spend so much time dwelling on the evidence of the Word that when the Devil comes and shows you contrary evidence, you can brush him off and say, "I have greater evidence than that. I have the Word of the living God, and I'm sticking with it."

If you'll do that, you'll not only bring honor and glory to God, you'll get what you ask for. Every single time.

Should You Ask or Appropriate?

Now that I've properly emphasized the importance of asking in the prayer of faith, I want to let you know there can be times when you are so confident of God's provision in a certain area that you won't have to ask at all. You will simply thank Him for it, believing you receive.

You may have meditated on what God says about healing, for instance, to the point where you are fully persuaded that healing is a part of your redemption rights. You know that you know that Jesus bore your sicknesses and carried your diseases two thousand years ago. You are fully assured that, spiritually, it is an established fact that by His stripes you *were* healed.

You know that healing is already yours, so when symptoms of sickness come, you don't have to ask God to heal you. You simply appropriate the healing that already belongs to you. You say, "Lord, I know that healing is mine because of what Jesus did for me on the cross. Therefore, I believe I receive that healing now. I thank You for it, in Jesus' name."

As I said earlier, some people pray that way just because they heard someone else do it. That's a mistake. You should only pray that way when you have the faith to do so.

In other words, pray the way that comes most naturally to you. If you can grab hold of something from God easier by asking Him for it, then ask. If it seems right to you just to appropriate, then do that. Don't worry about it. God won't chop your head off or throw your prayer out of heaven either way. Do whatever best enables you to release your faith and receive.

Both asking and appropriating are scriptural ways to receive from God. Take the prayer for wisdom for example. James 1:5 says that if you lack wisdom, you should ask for it. So asking is a scripturally acceptable way to release your faith to receive wisdom.

At the same time, however, 1 Corinthians 1:30 says that Jesus has already been made unto us wisdom. It's already ours in Him. So it's also acceptable to simply appropriate that wisdom by speaking words of faith and saying, "I thank You, Lord, that Jesus has been made unto me wisdom. I believe I have that wisdom now in His name."

Generally speaking, you won't start out appropriating. You'll grow into that. I think of it this way. A child asks. An older son or daughter appropriates. They are adult enough to know that their father has made certain things available to them and they are theirs for the taking.

You can see that in the story of the prodigal son in Luke 15. In verse 12, we find the younger son coming and *asking* his father for his part of the inheritance. He said, **Father, give me the portion of goods that falleth to me.**

Later in the story, we see the older son getting huffy about that. He was angry that his brother had squandered his inheritance, come home and been received by his father with open arms. So he complained to his father and said, **Lo, these many years do I serve thee, neither transgressed I at any time thy commandment: and yet thou never gavest me a kid, that I might make merry with my friends** (v. 29).

Do you know what the father said to the older son in response? He said, **Son, thou art ever with me, and all that I have is thine** (v. 31). In plain talk, he was saying, "Boy, you don't have to ask me for a calf. You can have a party anytime you want. Go kill your calf. Invite your friends. You don't have to ask me. Just take it."

In both of these cases, each of the sons could have had what belonged to them. It's just that the younger son had to ask and the elder one could just take.

"Well, I don't know if I'm a child or a son!"

Don't worry about it. If you're like most people, you'll be a child in one area and a son in another. You may be more developed in receiving healing, for instance, than you are in receiving finances. So don't try to get all clinical about it. Just do what comes easiest to you.

Who Can Use the Prayer of Faith?

We've already established that you can only use the prayer of faith in a situation where the will of God is clearly known. So you already understand when you can use this kind of prayer effectively.

But there's another important question we still need to answer: *Who can you pray the prayer of faith for?*

Of course, you can always pray this prayer for yourself. This prayer works great when you need to pray for the situations in your own life. But can you pray this prayer effectively for others?

Yes… and no.

Over the years, as we've prayed with people, we've discovered that you can pray the prayer of faith for a new Christian, a spiritual baby, so to speak—and see wonderful results. Usually these people aren't developed enough in the Word of God to have much faith of their own. They may not even know what God says about their situations. So God is gracious and allows more mature believers to use their faith to carry these babies for a while.

Actually, this is true not only of spiritual children, but of natural children as well. Parents can get powerful results by praying the prayer of faith for their children. I know that because my parents did it for me when I was young.

Sometimes I was glad. Sometimes I wasn't. There were times when I'd have a fever or a sore throat and I really wanted to stay sick for a little while. I thought it would be fun to stay home from school. But my parents would just say, "No, we'll take care of that." Then they'd lay hands on me, pray the prayer of faith for my healing and, sure enough, the Lord would raise me up and I'd have to go to school.

Once children begin to grow up, however, they have to start using their own faith. Instead of praying the prayer of faith for them, you'll have to use the prayer of agreement. God will insist on it because He wants them to grow up and be responsible. He won't allow them to lean on you all of their lives.

God doesn't want us to remain spiritual children. He wants us to grow up and start taking some spiritual responsibility. Jesus died on the cross and rose again so that we could become sons and daughters of God. He paid a tremendous price so we could be joint heirs with Him. He paid that price in vain if we refuse to take our place as sons and daughters.

So after we've been born again a while, God will stop allowing us to ride along on the spiritual shoulders of other people. He'll say to them, "Put that big baby down and let him learn to walk. Tell him to study the Word and find out for himself what My will is in that area of his life. Tell him to develop his own faith. It's time he began to act like a son."

Giving the Faith Command

Now that we've studied the prayer of faith, let's look at Mark 11 again and examine the command of faith. Jesus Himself sets the example for us. In that chapter, we see Him on the way home from a long day in Jerusalem. He's tired and hungry.

> And seeing a fig tree afar off having leaves, he came, if haply he might find any thing thereon: and when he came to it, he found nothing but leaves; for the time of figs was not yet. And Jesus answered and said unto it, No man eat fruit of thee hereafter for ever.
>
> And his disciples heard it. And in the morning, as they passed by, they saw the fig tree dried up from the roots. And Peter calling to remembrance saith unto him, Master, behold, the fig tree which thou cursedst is withered away.
>
> And Jesus answering saith unto them, Have faith in God. For verily I say unto you, That whosoever shall say unto this mountain, Be thou removed, and be thou cast into the sea; and shall not doubt in his heart, but shall believe that those things which he saith shall come to pass; he shall have whatsoever he saith.

MARK 11:13,14, 20-23

As you can see there, the command of faith is quite different than the prayer of faith. When you give the command of faith, you are not asking God for anything. You're not giving thanks to God. You aren't speaking to God at all. You are speaking to the thing or situation that needs to be changed. You are ordering it to obey the word of the Lord which is being spoken by you.

The command of faith can be given effectively only by a person who has a conscious revelation of the authority God has given him. It works only when you know who you are in Christ Jesus and you are absolutely certain the situation you are speaking to must obey you just as surely as it would have to obey Him if He spoke to it Himself.

The command of faith is not a request. It is not a prayer. It is not a plea. You do not beg mountains to be removed. You order them to be removed.

One of the best examples of the command of faith I've ever heard is that of a traveling minister who received a message while he was preaching a meeting many miles from home that his daughter was suffering from an abnormal growth on her eye. The growth had grown so large that if God didn't intervene quickly, something was going to have to be done medically to correct it.

This particular minister preached primarily about divine healing. He'd walked in divine health himself for many years and, because of his faith and the faith of his wife, his children had too. They'd never had to visit the doctor because of illness in their lives.

You might think that a man of God like this one who was so familiar with God's power to heal would jump right up and go to spitting and shouting and commanding in a situation like that, but he didn't. Instead, he folded the message up and put it in his pocket. He dismissed the situation from his mind so that he wouldn't be distracted by it while he preached his services during the day, and he determined that he would deal with it that night.

After the last service was over, this minister went to his room and opened his Bible. One by one, he began meditating on the healing Scriptures he knew so well. Isn't that amazing? Here was a man who preached and ministered healing day in and day out. A man who had himself been raised up supernaturally from a deathbed. A man who had lived in divine health for many years. Yet he felt it was necessary to take time to meditate on what the Bible said about healing before he addressed this situation.

He spent most of the night on those verses. He'd read and meditate on them an hour, then he'd sleep an hour. Then he'd read and meditate some more. By the time the night was spent, he was ready. His heart was full of faith. He knew that growth had to leave his daughter. So he simply cursed that thing and told it to go.

Then he sent a message to his daughter and said, "It's done."

Sure enough, the growth disappeared.

Notice this minister didn't spend much time speaking to that growth. He didn't put a lot of effort into it. He put the time and effort into meditating on the Word. He put the work into the preparation. So when he spoke, it was easy.

Learn a lesson from that. And the next time you get a bad report, don't jump up and start shouting at the mountain. Don't chant at it and start flailing around trying to push it down. Don't even try to pray real hard.

Just chill out!

Here's why. Usually in situations like that, your first response comes not out of your spirit, but out of your soul. You may be hollering the right words. You may be saying, "I curse that thing! I curse it! I believe it's gone! I believe it's gone!" but the panic in your voice indicates you aren't believing that at all.

What you need to do at those times is relax for a while and switch from your soul to your spirit. I used to know some people who owned the kind of pickup trucks that had two gas tanks. Are you familiar with those? At the flip of a switch they could change tanks. They could stop operating off the fuel in one tank and start operating off the fuel in the other.

Spiritually speaking, that's what you do when you draw near to God and begin meditating on His Word in a situation like that. When you abide in His Word and let His Word abide in you, you switch from the superficial fuel of the soul to the high-octane fuel of the Spirit. When you're operating off a full tank of that kind of faith fuel, you can speak to the mountain calmly, authoritatively, and it will move!

This may sound funny, but I believe you'll know what I mean when I say it: Never let the mountain see you cry.

In other words, never try to address the Devil or any circumstance he has brought your way when you are feeling weak and upset. Don't bawl and squawl while you're telling the Devil to flee from you. Don't ever let him see you like that. When you deal with mountains and devils, you act like a victorious son of God. You come at him as more than a conqueror.

It's all right for God to see you cry. He's your Father. If you need to take some time and just talk to Him about how much this situation has hurt you, then go ahead. That's appropriate. But don't go out of the throne room that way. You get settled on His Word first. You get established in His love and His power. Find your resting place in Him.

Don't be in such a rush. Spend some time waiting before God and getting things straight in your heart and mind before you try to deal with the situation. As Isaiah 40:31 says, **They that wait upon the Lord shall renew their strength; they shall mount up with wings as eagles; they shall run, and not be weary; and they shall walk, and not faint.** When you wait on the Lord, you actually entwine yourself with God and braid His Word into your being so thoroughly that nothing can separate you from His promises.

When you wait on the Lord, you exchange *your* strength for *His* strength. So when you step out to deal with the situation, you're using His power, not your own.

If you'll do that when you speak to the mountain, you'll be cool, calm and collected. That thing can scream in your face and you'll just answer it right back and say, "Scream if you want, but do it going out the door because I'm commanding you to leave and leave now, so you're out of here."

Pray First, Say Later

Although we don't see Jesus waiting on the Lord or praying about the fig tree before he spoke to it in Mark 11, the Bible reveals that there were times when Jesus prayed about a situation before He gave the command of faith. One such time was when He dealt with the death of Lazarus.

If you'll read the account of this incident in John 11, you'll see some very interesting things there. One of them is how Jesus responded when He was notified of Lazarus' illness. Even though Lazarus and his sisters were some of Jesus' dearest friends, even though Jesus knew the serious nature of this illness, the Bible says **he abode two days still in the same place where he was** (v. 6).

Jesus didn't get in a panic. He didn't dash off to Lazarus' house in a rush. He didn't say to His disciples, "Come on, boys. No time to pray now. We've got to get to Lazarus fast before this situation gets out of hand!"

No, Jesus stayed right where He was.

What did He do during that time? The Bible doesn't say specifically, but one thing is clear. He spent some of that time talking to God about the situation with Lazarus. We know He did because He told the disciples about Lazarus' death before they went to see him. So we know that Jesus got that information from the Father.

We also know that during that time He received instructions about what to do in this situation. He prayed until He knew how this situation would turn out. We know that because when Lazarus' sister greeted Jesus and informed Him of Lazarus' death, Jesus answered by saying, **Thy brother shall rise again** (v. 23).

Finally, when Jesus is standing in front of Lazarus' tomb, we hear Him pray, **Father, I thank thee that thou hast heard me** (v. 41). Those were the first words of His prayer there, so obviously Jesus was referring to the praying He had done before He arrived at Lazarus' house.

Clearly, Jesus had already talked to God about this mountain of death that had set itself before Him. Now He was ready to speak to the mountain itself and He cried with a loud voice, **Lazarus, come forth** (v.43).

When He did, death itself bowed its knee.

In Acts 9, we see Peter following the same pattern. The new believers in Joppa sent for him because their beloved sister in the Lord, Dorcas, had died. When they brought him into the room where her body was laid, Peter sent them all out and, turning his back on the body of Dorcas, he prayed.

Then Peter **turning him to the body said, Tabitha, arise. And she opened her eyes: and when she saw Peter, she sat up** (v. 40).

Peter prayed. Then he gave the faith command.

Once again, the mountain was removed and cast into the sea.

7

The Prayer of Agreement

"Again I say to you that if two of you agree
on earth concerning anything that they ask,
it will be done for them by My Father in heaven.
For where two or three are gathered together
in My name, I am there in the midst of them."

MATTHEW 18:19-20 NKJV

One of the most powerful prayers on earth for bringing about change is the prayer of agreement. Sadly, it is also the least understood and the most abused prayer. So let's start out on solid scriptural ground by looking at that Scripture again, this time from *The Amplified Bible*.

Again I tell you if two of you on earth agree (harmonize together, together make a symphony) about—anything

and everything—whatever they shall ask, it will come to pass and be done for them by My Father in heaven.

MATTHEW 18:19, 20 AMP

Notice, this translation tells us that when we pray the prayer of agreement, we should make a symphony with our prayers. Have you ever heard a symphony warming up with each player going in his own direction? It's terrible! Yet we've all heard prayers like that. They sound like an orchestra of instruments, each being played in a different key.

How can we tune up our prayers of agreement? There's only one way. We must make sure that every player—or in this case, pray-er—is following the same Conductor. The Holy Spirit will orchestrate if we will follow His lead.

A Threefold Cord Is Not Easily Broken

Before we delve into how to make our prayers a symphony, let's review why the prayer of agreement is so powerful. The answer is found in Deuteronomy 32:30 NKJV: **How could one chase a thousand, and two put ten thousand to flight, unless their Rock had sold them, and the Lord had surrendered them?**

It's not that you can't pray by yourself. You can, and the prayer of faith is a powerful way to pray. But, when two or more people truly pray in agreement, it multiplies their prayer power by staggering proportions.

That is one reason why God established marriage and families. A family in agreement is one of the most potent spiritual forces on earth. That's also the reason Satan's top priority is to break down marriages and tear families apart. He knows the devastating power of their agreement.

Ecclesiastes 4 reveals other benefits of the prayer of agreement.

> Two are better than one, because they have a good reward for their labor. For if they fall, one will lift up his companion.
>
> But woe to him who is alone when he falls, for he has no one to help him up.
>
> Again, if two lie down together, they will keep warm; but how can one be warm alone?
>
> Though one may be overpowered by another, two can withstand him. and a threefold cord is not quickly broken.

ECCLESIASTES 4:9-12 NKJV

The Amplified translation says, **They have a good [more satisfying] reward for their labor.** Obviously, one person could pray and get results, but it will be more rewarding to have someone share the victory.

Scotching

Actually, I got a mental picture of what the prayer of agreement can do when I saw a man parking a tow truck recently. After he'd parked it, he "scotched" his tire by pushing a block of wood behind the tire so it wouldn't roll. The prayer of agreement works spiritually much like that block of wood does naturally. It holds you in place. If I'm in prayer agreement with my husband, and the Devil starts applying great pressure, I could roll off my place of faith. But my husband will scotch that. He'll say, "No, I'm in agreement with you. God said...."

Some years ago, I had a friend who needed just that kind of help. She wanted to have children, but her faith was under pressure because she had experienced great tragedy in that area of her life. The first time she'd been pregnant, she'd given birth to a beautiful, healthy baby, but as soon as it was born, it died. The doctors couldn't find anything wrong with it. Later, she'd conceived again and delivered a marvelously healthy child. Again, it died shortly after birth.

You can imagine how she felt. She desperately wanted children, but she was afraid to have another one for fear of losing it. This situation required the prayer of agreement. "Before you ever try again," I told them, "we're going to cover all the bases and confirm what we believe. We'll build a platform from the Word of God."

We lived in different states, but we got together and made a ceremony out of it. We wrote down everything that we were going to believe: It would be a healthy pregnancy, the baby would be born full term, the baby would be healthy, and the baby would live.

We found our scriptural promises and built a platform from which to believe. Finally, we wrote it all down, then dated and signed it. Having done this, we prayed in harmony together.

In time she conceived and we rejoiced, reminding one another, "We agreed." She went in for her regular checkup, and the doctor began to run test after test. Finally, she was told, "You've got lupus."

When she called me, she was tempted to roll off her place of faith. I scotched that. "No," I said, "we agreed on a healthy pregnancy. Lupus would mean an unhealthy pregnancy." The doctors ran more tests and said, "You had lupus, but you don't have it now. We don't know where it went."

During another visit she was told, "This baby has Down's syndrome." They had to cancel their vacation, and the doctors wanted to abort the baby. I scotched that. "No, we agreed," I said. "Get out your contract. Nothing is going to be wrong with this child because we agreed." When she refused an abortion, the doctors ran more tests and said, "This child is fine." They were perplexed.

Just before she was due to deliver, she was in a car wreck, and the steering wheel hit her from the front. We got out our contract again and reviewed our stand. Healthy pregnancy. Full-term delivery. Healthy baby that will live and not die.

A short while later she gave birth to a healthy baby boy who did not die, but lived. The prayer of agreement works because a threefold cord is not easily broken. If you have agreement between yourself, another person and God, never give up.

Keys to the Prayer of Agreement

To more thoroughly understand the prayer of agreement, let's examine the scriptural keys that make it work. First of all, notice that the Bible says, **if two of you agree on earth.** The first thing that shows us is that you must be in agreement. Real agreement doesn't just mean mental assent. It's much deeper than that. It is a heart connection where two or more people are truly believing the same thing. (We'll see more about how to make that heart connection in a moment.)

The next scriptural guideline for the prayer of agreement is being on earth. Notice it doesn't say you have to agree in the same city or the same state. You don't even have to be in the same nation. Many times you'll be praying over a hot spot in crisis somewhere in the world, and God has orchestrated someone else to pray and believe the same thing elsewhere in the world. That is agreement, even though we aren't aware of it at the time. It is a two-part harmony being conducted by the Holy Spirit.

Another key word in this verse is *ask*. Notice that it doesn't say that if two of you agree on earth, your prayers will be answered. It says that if you agree, **Anything that they ask, it will be done for them.**

Too often I hear the prayer of agreement used this way. "Would you please agree with me for my new job?" someone asks.

"I agree!" the other person promises.

"Thank you, Father, for my new job!"

There was no asking involved in that transaction, except asking the other person. It was simple agreement between two people. God wasn't even asked to be a part of it.

God doesn't have a different definition for asking than we do. For instance, if I wanted you to give me a Bible, I wouldn't walk up to you and say, "Thank you for the Bible."

There is no secret formula to asking. You simply have to ask God for His involvement in your needs. James 4:2 says, **Ye have not because ye ask not.** The simple truth is that many times prayers aren't effective because no one bothered to ask God.

Asking means to make a request, to seek to obtain by making one's wants known. Then, when you've asked, thank Him!

Making the Connection

As I said before, the prayer of agreement will not produce results unless there is a heart connection of genuine agreement between both parties. That kind of connection isn't made quickly or flippantly. If it is, it will be, at best, ineffective. And, at worst, it will be downright destructive.

I once had someone ask me, "Will you agree with me? I'm in dire straights." Thank God, I knew better than to say, "Yes." If I'd agreed with them that their situation was dire, they would have been worse off—not better.

On another occasion, a woman asked me to agree with her for a financial breakthrough. "Okay," I said, "but we're not going to pray today." I've discovered that praying before you're in faith will frustrate your prayer life. "What verse of Scripture are you standing on?" I asked.

She got a blank look on her face. "Well...I need...."

I couldn't get in agreement with her right then because she didn't know her own spiritual stand. You never want to condemn people in this type of situation. You want to help stimulate their faith. If you pray prematurely, you're just clamoring. Rather than joining in as they flail their spiritual arms in prayer, help them to calm down and establish themselves on the Word of God. Spend the time with them that it takes to build a scriptural platform for their request. Then, when they know squarely where they stand and what they are believing for, you can pray in agreement with them.

It's also important that you get a sense that the person desiring your agreement isn't basing their prayers on what they've heard about prayer. Faith doesn't come by prayer. It comes by hearing the Word of God. In the situations I just described, it was crucial that I didn't agree with those people about their dire predicaments. What brought results was that we agreed on God's promises to provide what they needed to escape those predicaments!

Before you can ever pray the prayer of agreement, you must determine that you have the scriptural right to make the request. Are there any promises in the Bible that give you the right to ask that? If there is no scriptural support for your request, there is no point in going any further.

I've had people ask me to agree for something when they've stretched the Scripture far beyond God's intended meaning. In those situations, never lie and say, "All right, I'll agree." If you do, the prayer will not be answered, and you will have frustrated your own faith.

There will also be times when someone will ask you to pray the prayer of agreement and there is no way you can agree with their request. I've had people ask me to agree that they could marry someone else's husband or wife. You simply cannot pretend to agree. It will frustrate their faith as well as your own. Remember, you should be expecting to see 100 percent of your prayers answered. Don't set yourself up for failure.

Confidence Before God

There have been times when someone wanted to pray the prayer of agreement with me, but they needed help to bolster their confidence. Often, the reason they don't have confidence before God is that there is sin in their life. In that instance, they are scared to pray on their own, because they've fallen short of the mark. It won't work for you to go boldly before the throne of God while the person you're agreeing with is hanging out in the parking lot.

In that instance, before the prayer of agreement can be prayed, you need to show them scriptural proof that the blood of Jesus washes away all sin. Lead them in repentance. You don't have to agree that they're in sin. Agree with them that they are righteous before God because of the Cross.

Sometimes I ask people, "Do you have the right to ask that?" Let them go over the reasons that they do have the right. It will make their approach more bold. "Yes, I do," they'll say. "I've not been perfect all of my life, but my sins are under the blood."

Or perhaps they'll answer, "Well, I don't have the right to ask because…." My response is, "Okay, let's go boldly and obtain mercy from God. While we're there, we'll get what you need."

Don't let things be nebulous. Do actual business with God. If you practice that yourself, it will be easier for you to help other people the same way.

Locate Their Faith

Before you jump headfirst into prayer agreement, it's a good idea to make sure you're on the same page in every area. For instance, you may have the faith for someone to receive divine healing without surgery, but what will happen if you jump out to agree with them only to discover that they're believing for a successful surgery?

Take the time to locate exactly what they can believe. Then jump in with them right where they are. Never make them feel intimidated in their place of faith. There is no trick to locating someone's level of faith. Simply ask them—they know what they believe. I often ask, "What is it that you can believe without any trouble?" Remember, God can do exceedingly abundantly above all that they ask or think. Never doubt that He will do more for them than they ask.

It's not a good idea for someone to try and stretch their faith out of measure. They won't get their prayer answered, and it will hurt their faith. Go ahead and get them to start using the faith that they have, and they'll see results. You can agree with them for something better the next time. That way their faith is bolstered.

Always remember, this prayer involves very distinct, understood agreement. It's a definite request. It doesn't involve groaning and travail, and it doesn't have to be a long prayer. According to Philippians 4:6 NKJV, **Be anxious for nothing, but in everything by prayer and supplication, with thanksgiving, let your requests be made known to God.**

The Amplified translations says, with **definite requests**. That means your request can't be nebulous, and it can't be in tongues. The prayer of agreement must be prayed with your understanding. There are other kinds of prayer that involve waiting on God and praying in other tongues. But when it comes to the prayer of agreement, don't ramble. Decide what you can receive through the promises of the Holy Scripture; then go boldly before God and make a definite request.

The power of God will be released on your behalf.

8

The Prayer of Supplication

*Praying always with all prayer and supplication
in the Spirit, and watching thereunto with all
perseverance and supplication for all saints.*

EPHESIANS 6:18

The prayer of supplication, like many kinds of prayer, is a prayer in which a believer asks for something. But the prayer of supplication differs in one important way. It is more intense, more heart-wrenching than almost any other kind of prayer.

If you've ever read about people whose prayers ushered in a great move of God, then you have an idea of the intensity of supplication. The word *supplication* means an earnest entreaty with heartfelt fervency. It involves not only the spirit, but the soul of the person praying. The pray-er who supplicates doesn't just desire the thing he is asking for; he is desperate for it. He is crying out to God with every atom of his being.

Supplication is not a little "God bless you" type of prayer. It is never casual or off-the-cuff. Rather, it is an earnest, serious prayer that the Bible commands us to pray.

In Philippians 4:6, for example, Paul instructs us to **be careful for nothing; but in every thing by prayer and supplication with thanksgiving let your requests be made known unto God.** And in 1 Timothy 2:1-2, he tells us to make **supplications, prayers, intercessions, and giving of thanks,...for all men; for kings, and for all that are in authority; that we may lead a quiet and peaceable life in all godliness and honesty.**

Psalm 27 gives us a sense of what the prayer of supplication sounds like. There, David prays:

> **The Lord is my light and my salvation; whom shall I fear? the Lord is the strength of my life; of whom shall I be afraid? When the wicked, even mine enemies and my foes, came upon me to eat up my flesh, they stumbled and fell. Though an host should encamp against me, my heart shall not fear: though war should rise against me, in this will I be confident.**
>
> **One thing have I desired of the Lord, that will I seek after; that I may dwell in the house of the Lord all the days of my life, to behold the beauty of the Lord, and to inquire in his temple.**

PSALM 27:1-4

The fervency of this prayer comes across even more clearly in the Amplified version: **One thing have I asked of the Lord, that I will seek after, inquire for, and [insistently] require, that I may dwell in the house of the Lord [in His presence] all** the days of my life, to behold and gaze upon the beauty [the sweet attractiveness and the delightful loveliness] of the Lord, and to meditate, consider and inquire in His temple. Hear, O Lord, when I cry aloud: have mercy and be gracious to me and answer me! (vv. 4,7).

You can see that David wasn't praying a casual prayer there. He was crying out to the Lord, longing for the presence of God in his life. He so longed and yearned for it, that it came out of his heart in desperation.

Ask for Rain

We find another example of supplication in Zechariah 10:1. **Ask ye of the Lord rain in the time of the latter rain; so the Lord shall make bright clouds, and give them showers of rain, to every one grass in the field.** The word *ask* in this verse is not a casual request. This doesn't mean that you say, "Lord, I'm asking You for the rain." Although we do ask Him that way at times, this is not what the Lord was saying here. This word *ask* means, "You won't be happy until you see it done." There is a desperation with this kind of asking. It is like grabbing hold of something and refusing to let go because you have to have it.

The story about Hannah in 1 Samuel gives us another excellent example of fervent supplication. Hannah was a barren but godly woman who longed to have children. Eventually, her desire for a child became so great that she lifted it up to God with tremendous fervency.

> And she was in bitterness of soul, and prayed unto the Lord, and wept sore. And she vowed a vow, and said, O Lord of hosts, if thou wilt indeed look on the affliction of thine handmaid, and remember me, and not forget thine handmaid, but wilt give unto thine handmaid a man child, then I will give him unto the Lord all the days of his life, and there shall no razor come upon his head.
>
> And it came to pass, as she continued praying before the Lord, that Eli marked her mouth. Now Hannah, she spake in her heart; only her lips moved, but her voice was not heard: therefore Eli thought she had been drunken.
>
> And Eli said unto her, How long wilt thou be drunken? put away thy wine from thee.
>
> And Hannah answered and said, No, my lord, I am a woman of a sorrowful spirit: I have drunk neither wine nor strong drink, but have poured out my soul before the Lord. Count not thine handmaid for a daughter of Belial: for out of the abundance of my complaint and grief have I spoken hitherto.
>
> Then Eli answered and said, Go in peace: and the God of Israel grant thee thy petition that thou hast asked of him.
>
> 1 SAMUEL 1:10-17

God had always desired for Hannah to have children, and she may have asked Him to give them to her many times. But the answer to that prayer was withheld until the intensity of her desire grew to be so great, she could hardly bear it. It became a burning fire inside of her. What did she do with that desperate longing and deep desire? She went to the temple and lifted it up to God in earnest entreaty.

Her heart was so burdened, she couldn't even speak out loud. Only her lips moved. So we see that supplication doesn't have to be loud praying, but it does have to come from the depths of your heart.

Cultivating Your Desires

One time, a man came up to me after a service and said, "I'm so concerned about myself. My prayers are so shallow, I get embarrassed before God."

I knew exactly what the man was going through. There are times when we all feel exactly the same way. When you're in that condition and you hear someone praying fervently, you could easily mistake it for emotionalism. But supplication isn't emotionalism and it isn't a personality quirk. It does, however, say something about the person's heart and their sensitivity to the Holy Spirit.

When people pray fervently, it's because there is a great desire in their hearts. Where did they get that kind of burning desire? From God!

"Why hasn't God given me that kind of desire?" you may ask.

He has—but you haven't noticed it. You see, it doesn't begin as a great, burning burden of prayer. It begins as a tiny flicker. Then, as you fan that first little flame by giving attention to it in the Word and in prayer, it grows.

If you make the mistake of ignoring or suppressing that initial desire, it will fade away. So don't do that! That tiny seed of desire is your cue from the Holy Spirit about the direction He wants you to take in your prayers.

When it comes to your heart, grab hold of it and lift it up to God. If, for instance, you find yourself wishing for revival to break out in your church, say, "Lord, I'd like us to experience revival." That request may sound small and weak at first, but speak it out anyway. Don't let it sit on the inside of you. Do something with it.

Once you take the first step, God will take the second. He may cause you to stumble across a book about revival that will stir you up and increase your desire even more. He'll guide you to Scriptures that promise revival so you can begin to ask in faith.

In some ways, supplication reminds me of taking care of a garden. You plant tiny little seeds, and keep turning up the dirt all around them. You water and protect them until they grow to their full capacity.

Desire for the things of God starts in a Christian's life in the same way—the desire for rain; the desire to see people healed; the desire to move in the gifts of the Spirit; the desire to win souls for Jesus. Each desire is like a little spark of divine life. If you'll cultivate it, turn it over and lift it to the Lord, it will grow and mature.

Each time you lift up that request to God, He'll move on your heart, and the desire to see that prayer answered will grow stronger. If you keep that cycle going, eventually, like Hannah, you'll become so fervent in your request that the Devil himself won't be able to stop you from getting what you want.

Back in the early 1950s, Brother Kenneth E. Hagin proved this process in his own prayer life when he began to develop a curiosity about the power gifts. Initially, his curiosity was just a little flicker on the inside of him so he began studying about them in the Bible. He studied the working of miracles, gifts of healing and special faith. He started right where he was—at the point of curiosity—and began lifting it up to the Lord. Day after day, he studied the Word and lifted up his growing desire to see the power gifts operate once again in the Church.

Before long that desire grew so intense that, when he went to bed each night, he left a blanket out in the other room because he knew he'd be getting out of bed in the middle of the night to pray about that desire. Each time, God blessed his desire and gave it back to him. It continued to grow until it became so fervent that the power gifts were an absolute requirement for him. His supplications became as heartfelt as David's were in Psalm 27. Of course, God answered his supplication, and the power gifts began manifesting in his ministry.

God's Ways

In Isaiah 55, we see a scriptural illustration of this cycle. It begins with verse 8 where the Lord said, **My thoughts are not your thoughts, neither are your ways my ways.** There God is speaking about natural, unregenerate people. They don't think like God. They can't think what He thinks or desire what He desires because they live in spiritual darkness.

It would be terrible if that were all God had to say on the matter of His thoughts and ways. But, thank God, He didn't leave us there. Once we're born again, God comes to live inside us. We're joined to Him by His Spirit and He can begin to send off flashes of insight to us. He can begin to prompt us to think His thoughts and desire His desires. Those thoughts and ways are above our natural thoughts and ways. In fact, this passage says,

> As the heavens are higher than the earth, so are my ways higher than your ways, and my thoughts than your thoughts.
>
> For as the rain cometh down, and the snow from heaven, and returneth not thither, but watereth the earth, and maketh it bring forth and bud, that it may give seed to the sower, and bread to the eater: so shall my word be that goeth forth out of my mouth: it shall not return unto me void, but it shall accomplish that which I please, and it shall prosper in the thing whereto I sent it.

vv. 9-11

Notice He said, "As the rain and snow came down from heaven...so shall my word be." Those words reveal the fact that all Spirit-inspired prayer originates with God. It doesn't originate on earth. God starts the cycle of prayer Himself by flashing one of His thoughts into our heart. We pick up on that thought and, like the rain that waters the earth and then returns to heaven, we return that thought to God by speaking it back to Him in prayer.

The primary way God sends His thoughts to us is through His written Word. For instance, in 1 Peter 2:24 NKJV, God gives us His thought about sickness by saying, **By His [Jesus'] stripes, you [are] healed.** When sickness attacks your body, the Holy Spirit will quicken that thought to you and you'll lift it back to Him in prayer.

When you first hear about healing, you might begin with only an inquiry. You might just lift that thought from 1 Peter 2:24 back up to God by saying, "Lord, I want to believe what that verse says, but my denomination taught me that healing had passed away. Would You show me more about that? Is it truly Your will to heal me now?"

God will answer that prayer and cause it to prosper by leading you to other Scriptures. **I am the Lord that healeth thee...who healeth all thy diseases. He sent his word and healed them, and delivered them from their destructions** (Exodus 15:26, Psalm 103:3; 107:20).

Remember this: no thought of your healing, prosperity or even salvation originated with you. God gave you those thoughts. Your responsibility is to pray back to Him His desire for you.

Why can't God just go *Ping!* and heal everyone on earth? He certainly has the power! The Bible says that there is a river of life flowing from the throne of God. That river has more than enough life for the world. Yet God designed a plan that required man to first receive a desire from God and then start wanting it as much as God wants it. God made asking and receiving a spiritual law. So He can't do anything without involving man.

Remember blind Bartimaeus? He proved that. He cried out, "Jesus, son of David, have mercy on me! Jesus, son of David, have mercy on me!" He was clearly blind, and his need was apparent. Yet Jesus couldn't heal him until he made his request.

In those days, certain blind men wore cloaks to identify themselves. The Bible says that Bartimaeus threw off his cloak before Jesus ever touched him. So we know that he had faith to be healed. Even so, Jesus asked, "What do you want?"

If I'd been Bartimaeus, I might have been tempted to say, "What do You mean, Jesus? Can't You see that I'm blind? Are You blind yourself?" But, thank God, Bartimaeus didn't say that. Instead, he asked for what he wanted. He said, **Lord, that I might receive my sight.... And immediately he received his sight, and followed Jesus in the way** (Mark 10:51,52).

Depend on the Holy Spirit

Don't you know that when Bartimaeus answered Jesus that day, it was with a fervent, heartfelt cry? Can't you just hear him crying out, "Lord! That I may receive my sight!" Those words were backed by hours, days and years of longing and desire. I don't know why there's such power in that kind of desire—but there is.

That's why when God said in Zechariah 10:1, **Ask ye of the Lord rain,** He wasn't telling us to make a casual request. He wanted us to develop a yearning in our soul for the rain. He wanted us to have a desperation, a fervency and a heated desire for the outpouring of His Spirit.

We may pray, but are our prayers too cold? How full and laden with desire are they? Does it really make a difference to you about the rain? Or are you indifferent? What about healing? What about souls for the harvest?

God has a tremendous desire for men to be saved. He is waiting for the precious fruit of the earth. Think how He longs after souls. There is an amazing yearning in His heart in this day and hour. He needs us to share that yearning.

How can we do it? By depending on the Holy Spirit. The Bible calls Him the **Spirit of grace** (Heb. 10:29) and supplication . He is living on the inside of you, and He will help you supplicate. (Rom. 8:26.) He is fervent, and He'll help your prayers to be fervent.

I hardly ever go to the Father without talking to Him about the desire for souls. But the fact is, God has many other desires, too. So look in your own heart and fan the flame of desire that God has planted there. It may be for your son or daughter to get right with God. It may be for the plan of God to be fulfilled in your life. It may be for Christians to be changed more and more into the image of Jesus. It may be a desire to free men from demonic bondage.

Whatever the desire in your heart, begin lifting it up to God. As you do, the Holy Spirit will stir up supplication in you. You can never pray the prayer of supplication without the Holy Spirit. That's why it's crucial that you learn to lean on Him.

One of the pitfalls of people who pray is that they begin leaning on what they know and understand. Eventually, they'll put their faith in their prayers rather than in God. That is a real trap where prayer is concerned, because prayer can get more religious than any other practice in Christianity.

So never think you'll be heard by God because of how much you pray. You'll be heard when you pray right. And don't depend on notes you've taken from some great sermon. Don't depend on what you read in this book. Depend on the Holy Ghost. Make it your goal every day of your life to be sensitive to Him.

Don't Let the Devil Drive You

There is one thing I want to warn you about. It's the fleshly fervency that comes just because some circumstance has stirred your natural soul. We see this kind of fervency in prayer groups a lot. If you say, "Brother So-and-so needs prayer," people will pray halfheartedly. But if someone gives the gory details of the car wreck that brother was in, everyone will pray really hard.

"What's wrong with that?" you might ask. I'll tell you what's wrong with it. That kind of fervency isn't inspired by what the Holy Spirit is doing on the inside of you; it's triggered by what the Devil is doing on the outside. Who do you want to drive your prayer life? The Holy Ghost or the Devil? If you allow crisis situations and gory details to motivate your prayers, then the Devil will tie up your prayer life by keeping you busy trying to put out fires.

If the Christians praying over that gory wreck had been sensitive to the Holy Ghost, they would have picked up their cues *before* the car wreck and prayed that thing out so that it would never have happened. You can't do that if you're spending your time responding to the Devil. You hear about a fire he started in someone's life, and you pray about that. Then you hear something else dreadful, and you run to try to stomp it out. Finally, you're so tired, you don't pray again until you hear about another desperate situation.

God never designed prayer to be that way.

Your spirit is the candle of the Lord. He will give you your prayer impulses straight from heaven. The Holy Spirit will show you things to come. He'll show you what God is doing and what the Devil is going to attempt. Then He'll tell you exactly how to pray.

Listen to Your Heart

How can you start getting those messages from God? By praying in the Spirit and by doing other, very simple things. For instance, when someone comes to your mind, stop and pray for them! It doesn't have to be a long, drawn out prayer. Just let the Holy Spirit lead you.

I keep a prayer journal and write down the names of people whom God brings to my mind. Sometimes I just pray. Other times, the Lord will give me a Scripture for them, or He may direct me to phone them. It's important that we develop our ability to pray by the prompting of the Holy Ghost.

He has a better communications link with us than CNN or the Internet. He will make divine connections between you and anyone else in the world. The only limiting factor is your willingness to pick up His cues and follow His leading.

When I was a young girl, I started praying for Siberia, a region in Russia. I'd wake up in the night and pray for the saints in Siberia. I would see this young girl about my age and

I'd pray for her. I prayed for her for so many years that I felt as if she was a dear friend.

Years later, before glasnost, I was in Russia attending a meeting of the underground church. The meeting was overflowing with people. There were four girls there who had traveled by train across seven time zones from Siberia to worship with us. Throughout the meeting, I kept looking at one of the girls. Every time I looked at her, she was looking at me. There was something so familiar about her. I kept thinking, *I know that girl! But how could I?*

Then the Lord revealed to me that she was the girl for whom I'd prayed so long. When I told her that, we wept and cried together. We talked and shared our stories. She was a wonderful lady of God. Isn't it amazing how God can connect us if we'll let Him? Too often, we depend on our minds. We depend on letters. We depend on telephones. We depend on telegrams. But the Holy Ghost doesn't have need of them. He only has need of you and me. He needs us to pray in the Spirit.

In Ephesians 6:18, Paul says that if you'll pray in the Spirit, you can pray for *all* saints. You can pray for saints in the country you're going to visit. You don't even have to know their names. When you meet them, you'll know them by the inspiration of the Spirit of God. There will be a kindred spirit. You may have prayed them out of circumstances which could have resulted in their death several times, and they may have prayed for you.

Many times we've said, "I wish God would move on me." He is already moving! He's giving us those nudges and impulses. But we've grieved the Spirit by ignoring them.

Years ago, I read a book written by an old saint of God which said that the main lesson to be learned in prayer is, do it, do it, do it.

Use the Plumb Line

When it comes to responding to the promptings of your spirit, one thing you must remember is that those promptings, if they are truly of God, will always line up with the Word of God. The Word of God is the standard. It is the plumb line against which everything is to be measured.

Let the Word anchor your soul, especially in the area of supplication. People who pray prevailing prayers for cities, nations and people are so convinced of what they believe. Why? Not just because of the witness in their heart, but because that witness is backed up by the Word.

When you pray prevailing prayers, you can't pray them based on our word. You can't pray them based on someone else's word. You have to pray them because you've heard a word from God and you will not let it go.

That kind of anchoring makes you tenacious. Time only solidifies it, because every day that you wait to see your answer, you become more resolute. And as you become more resolute, you absolutely will not move. You know that God, His will and His Word are one, and you will not quit until you see them manifested on the earth.

That kind of tenacity is vital for success in supplication because you don't necessarily get the desire or the answer right away. As we said before, God will give you the desire in your heart, and you may have to return it to Him many times to get more desire. Eventually, you'll almost be consumed by that desire. It may seem as though the desire is bigger than you, because it is. You're carrying one of God's desires.

Sometimes that can be overwhelming. I was praying with a precious old saint of God one time, and my heart was so heavy with those kinds of desires, I didn't know what to do. She said the Lord showed her one time that she could put those things in her hand and lift them up to God. It was so childlike and simple that I started doing it. And it worked! I'd take things out of my heart, put them by faith in my hand and lift them up to God. Sure enough, I sensed a release. My heart was free!

Later, the Lord blessed me by revealing that what He had witnessed in the heart of that dear lady was scriptural. He showed me Lamentations 3:41: **Let us lift up our heart with our hands unto God in the heavens.** That is a powerful way to unburden your heart.

Prayer Belongs to God

One thing you must remember as your desire in supplication grows is that you are not praying to get God to do something. It's the other way around! God is leading you to pray so He can do something!

If you'll remember that, your faith will stay strong. A good example of this truth is found in Daniel 9. Daniel was in Babylonian captivity when he read in God's Word that the judgment for Jerusalem would last seventy years. Daniel realized that the time of judgment was up, and he said, "Hey, we should be going home!"

Notice, the idea that it was time for the Jews to go home didn't originate with Daniel. It was God's idea that He had declared through His prophet Jeremiah long before Daniel read it in Babylon. It was God's will to release the people. It was God's plan to release the people. It was God's time to release the people.

So why weren't they back in Jerusalem? Because God needed someone to pray. It was God who sparked Daniel to read that prophesy. It was God who witnessed in Daniel's heart to pray. But it was Daniel who prayed.

In the first year of his reign I Daniel understood by books the number of the years, whereof the word of the Lord came to Jeremiah the prophet, that he would accomplish seventy years in the desolations of Jerusalem.

And I set my face unto the Lord God, to seek by prayer and supplications, with fasting, and sackcloth, and ashes: And I prayed unto the Lord my God, and made my confession, and said, O Lord, the great and dreadful God, keeping the covenant and mercy to them that love him, and to them that keep his commandments; we have sinned, and have committed iniquity, and have done wickedly, and have rebelled, even by departing from thy precepts and from thy judgments: Neither have we hearkened unto thy servants the prophets, which spake in thy name to our kings, our princes, and our fathers, and to all the people of the land.

O Lord, righteousness belongeth unto thee, but unto us confusion of faces, as at this day; to the men of Judah, and to the inhabitants of Jerusalem, and unto all Israel, that are near, and...countries wither thou hast driven them, because of their trespass that they have trespassed against thee.

O Lord, to us belongeth confusion of face, to our kings, to our princes, and to our fathers, because we have sinned against thee.

To the Lord our God belong mercies and forgivenesses, though we have rebelled against him; Neither have we obeyed the voice of the Lord our God, to walk in his laws, which he set before us by his servants the prophets.

Yea, all Israel have they transgressed law, even by departing, that they might not obey thy voice; therefore the curse is poured upon us, and the oath that is written in the law of Moses the servant of God, because we have sinned against him.

And now, O Lord our God, that hast brought thy people forth with a mighty hand, and hast gotten thee renown, as at this day; we have sinned, we have done wickedly.

O Lord, according to all thy righteousness, I beseech thee, let thine anger and thy fury be turned away from thy city Jerusalem, thy holy mountain: because for our sins, and for the iniquities of our fathers, Jerusalem and thy people are become a reproach to all that are about us.

Now therefore, O our God, hear the prayer of thy servant, and his supplications, and cause thy face to shine upon thy sanctuary that is desolate, for the Lord's sake.

O my God, incline thine ear, and hear; open thine eyes, and behold our desolations, and the city which is called by thy name: for we do not present our supplications before thee for our righteousnesses, but for thy great mercies.

DANIEL 9:2-11,15-18

Beseeching God

We've already seen that the prayers of supplication can involve praying for yourself, for unbelievers, for saints and for the move of God. But here in Daniel's prayer, we see it can also include confession of sin. It can include "beseeching God," pleading for someone to receive a blessing they are not in a spiritual position to receive.

Notice, however, Daniel didn't say, "God, I beseech You. Look upon the sins of all those horrible Israelites and the people from Jerusalem who did not obey Your voice."

No, he used words like we and our. He said, "We have sinned and have committed iniquity. We have made no prayer before the Lord."

Identification

Think about that a moment. Here is Daniel, who is praying and seeking God's face. He prayed so much in Babylon that he was thrown in the lions' den. He clearly isn't one of those with confusion of face. He clearly isn't one of those prayerless sinners. Yet he identified himself with them.

That's the nature of supplication. It brings you to a place where you're standing with the people you're praying for. You're not standing apart from them in a high and lofty place. You're not pointing an accusing finger, saying, "What's wrong with these people?"

You'd never be able to help them that way. You'd only manage to accuse and intimidate them. How did Jesus lift us up? By identifying with us. He didn't stay in heaven and look down on us in accusation. He came and stood with us.

When you pray the prayer of supplication, you can confess your own sins and the sins of others with stunning results. There have been incredible instances of freedom that came when a person who had been abused and victimized by another prayed and asked God for mercy. They didn't just say, "God, I forgive them." That person who abused them needed a lot more than simply their forgiveness.

Remember when Jesus was hanging on the cross? He didn't pray, "Father, I forgive them, for they know not what they do."

He prayed, **Father,** [You] **forgive them** (Luke 23:34).

When Stephen was being stoned in Acts 7:60, the Bible says **And he kneeled down, and cried with a loud voice, Lord, lay not this sin to their charge. And when he had said this, he fell asleep.**

It wouldn't have done much good for Stephen to forgive his murderers. They needed God's forgiveness. They needed His mercy, but they weren't asking for it. So Stephen asked in their place.

It's always easy to look on greater sin and judge it, but it's humbling to identify with and confess the sin. Daniel was one man whose prayers of supplication released a whole people from captivity.

When you tap into the desires of God, your prayers will do the same.

9

The Prayer of Intercession

*And I sought for a man among them, that should
make up the hedge, and stand in the gap before
me for the land, that I should not destroy it:
but I found none...I exhort therefore, that,
first of all, supplications, prayers, intercessions,
and giving of thanks, be made for all men.*

EZEKIEL 22:30; 1 TIMOTHY 2:1

There are numerous misconceptions in the body of Christ about the prayer of intercession. Many Christians seem to think, for example, that intercession is the only kind of prayer. Sometimes people say, "God called me to be an intercessor." When I hear that, I always think, *No, He didn't. He called you to pray all kinds of prayer. Intercession is just one kind.*

"Oh, but intercession is the most important kind of prayer!" some may say.

That's not true either. The most important kind of prayer is the kind the Holy Ghost wants you to pray, because that's the only kind that will work. He will lead you to pray different kinds of prayers at different times because He, and only He, knows what kind of prayer will get the job done. Therefore, to be truly effective in prayer, you have to learn to flow with Him. You have to be flexible.

At times, I've been hesitant to teach on all kinds of prayer because when people categorize prayer, they tend to become clinical about it. Long before anyone had heard the words *supplication* and *intercession*, people were praying those prayers. Sadly, those same people often become stiff and unresponsive to the Holy Ghost once they've learned the different categories of prayer. They try to take matters into their own hands and decide intellectually which type of prayer to pray in which situation.

Studying different kinds of prayer helps because it will broaden your understanding and strengthen your faith when you pray. But always remember, studying prayer is very different from praying.

It's not difficult to separate the primary characteristics of supplication and intercession when you study. But when you're flowing in the Spirit, it's virtually impossible to tell when you move from supplication to intercession. So don't worry about that! Just flow with the Holy Spirit, and let Him decide where you're going. He will never lead you in the wrong way.

You've probably already noticed in the previous chapter that many of the prayers people have labeled as intercession are really prayers of supplication. Now that you know it, don't get superior with anyone. It's nice to have it right in your notebook, but what really counts is having it right on your knees.

Actually, there is an element of supplication within intercession, so you can't completely separate them. These kinds of prayers work together like the fingers of your hand. That's why you can't be clinical about it. You just have to flow with the Spirit. In other words, when the Holy Ghost starts moving on you to pray and you feel as though you want to weep, don't try to figure out whether you're supplicating or interceding. Just weep!

The Primary Ingredient

In our study of supplication, we found it had a mandatory ingredient. It's an ingredient that is absolutely imperative for the prayer of supplication to have power. What is that ingredient?

Desire. Without desire, the prayer of supplication will never get off the ground. It will not bring the necessary result.

In the same way, the prayer of intercession also has a mandatory ingredient. It is the ingredient of love. Effective, Holy Spirit-inspired intercession is born from love. Love is the driving force behind it. You so love those you intercede for that you cannot stop praying until they have what they need from God.

The love that fuels intercession is not just a feeling; it's an action. It causes us to love not in word only, but in deed. (1 John 3:18.)

Because it is motivated by fervent love, intercession, like supplication, can be more demonstrative in its expression than other kinds of prayer. It may be accompanied by weeping, groanings or sighing. It may be loud at times. Or it may be quiet.

Be that as it may, always remember that the important thing is not how you sound outwardly. What matters is that you're praying out of your heart. Don't watch someone else pray with strong crying and tears and think, *Oh, that's spiritual. I'm going to pray that way.* No, back up to the river of God that inspired those tears. Yield yourself to the Holy Spirit, and just pray from your heart. If it's not in your heart to cry, don't fake it. Faking it won't make you a good pray-er. It will make you religious. It will make you good at being flaky.

Whatever you pray, it needs to be heartfelt. If you'll get into the heart of God, I guarantee you that He'll start putting His love on the inside of you. When He does, you'll know it because His love is far superior to our own human love. God's love is selfless. When you love with His love, you don't care if your name is known. You don't need a sign over your door that says "Chief Intercessor." You don't care what people think about you. You just want to be a blessing.

God's love will also cause you to be moved with compassion. When you have compassion, you don't just pity someone who's in trouble; you suffer with them. Compassion doesn't just shake its head and say, "Isn't that a shame." It's far deeper than that. Compassion draws you so that you hurt because someone else hurts.

We've all known parents who are so compassionate toward a sick child that they would gladly take the child's pain if they could. Even before I had children, I had a dog that had trouble with her eyes, and she cried in pain. I couldn't stand it. When she would cry, so would I. The compassion I felt for my dog went way past "I'm so sorry that she's in pain." It caused me to feel that pain with her.

The love of God causes you to care so deeply about another's need that watching TV won't shut it out. Reading a good book won't make it go away. You weep with those who weep, and you rejoice with those who rejoice.

> Love endures long and is patient and kind: love never is envious nor boil over with jealousy; is not boastful or vainglorious, does not display itself haughtily.
>
> It is not conceited—arrogant and inflated with pride; it is not rude (unmannerly), and does not act unbecomingly. Love [God's love in us] does not insist on its own rights or its own way, for it is not self-seeking; it is not touchy or fretful or resentful; it takes no account of the evil done to it—it pays no attention to a suffered wrong;
>
> It does not rejoice at injustice and unrighteousness, but rejoices when right and truth prevail.

Love bears up under anything and everything that comes, is ever ready to believe the best of every person, its hopes are fadeless under all circumstances, and it endures everything [without weakening].

Love never fails.

1 Corinthians 13:4-8 AMP

Finish Your Course

I especially like that last verse: *Love never fails.* Love never quits until its job is finished. The New Testament speaks specifically of two people who finished their course, fulfilling their God-appointed destiny in life. Both of them were compelled by love. The first one was Jesus. Remember what He said on the cross? **It is finished** (John 19:30).

The second one who finished his course was Paul. He said, **I have finished my course** (2 Tim. 4:7).

There are many people who have started their courses. There are many who are in the middle of their courses. But there are few who finish their course. It's like running a marathon. A lot of people start, but not all of them go the whole distance.

What is the compelling force behind the ability to finish? Love. That's true in life, and it's true in prayer. So take a look at your own heart. What is motivating you to pray?

Many people are motivated by zeal. Zeal is a wonderful thing, but it will cool off. Zeal will never burn hot enough to sustain you through to the end. When you pray for a few months without seeing an answer, if all you had to begin with was zeal, you'll get weary and give up on those prayers. But love will heat you back up and get you praying again.

Love is the drive that motivates us to stay on our course. Jesus was moved by love. It moved Him from the cradle to the cross. It was love that put Him in motion.

It had the same effect on our heavenly Father. He so loved the world that He did something. He didn't just sit up in heaven and say, "Oh, how I love the world. We need to have a happy angel band write songs about it." No, He so loved the world that He moved. He made a literal, geographical move from heaven to earth.

Love will not just move your heart. It will start there, but as it grows and develops, it will move you to do something. You can always tell the people who are full of the love of God. They're on the move, and not just in the sight of other people. Love will move you out of bed and into your prayer closet early in the morning. Sometimes it will move you to put your fork down so you can fast and pray for someone. Sometimes it will move you to pull away and seek the fellowship of God until you get an answer for them. If you have the love of God, you will not be able to stay still in your Christian life. Love is so hot, it will move you.

One praying man who burned with that kind of love was David Brainerd. He was a physically weak, but spiritually powerful man of God who made a mark for God on this nation more than a hundred years ago. Brainerd lived for years in poor health, and he died at an early age from consumption.

In spite of failing health, he labored for the Lord among the Native Americans in the forests of northern Pennsylvania. On many a winter night, he went into the forest and knelt in the deep snow to pray. He interceded on behalf of the Indians until he was soaked with perspiration, despite the frigid temperatures.

God heard his prayers and sent a mighty revival among the Indians. Not only did God send that revival, but also in answer to Brainerd's prayers, He transformed Brainerd's father-in-law, Jonathan Edwards.

Edwards had been a mighty prince of metaphysics. He was probably one of the mightiest thinkers that America had ever produced. He was transformed into a flaming evangelist who preached on the subject of sinners in the hands of an angry God. Strong men in the audiences felt as if he preached until the floor of the church was falling out and they were sinking into hell. Many sprang from their seats and threw their arms around the pillars of the church while they cried to God for mercy.[1]

The kind of love and desire that drove an ailing man to his knees in deep snow can't be manufactured. It comes from the heart. If most of us tried to pray that way, we'd probably just catch a cold. What caused him to have such an incredible hunger for souls?

He didn't get it from a man. You can't get it from anyone except God. God has to work in your heart until you are unwilling to live without revival. You simply cannot survive without the answers to the prayers that love compels you to pray. When that desire is present, you don't really pay attention to the minutes and hours or to the demonstrations of the Spirit that happen during prayer. You are aware of love—and love alone.

Moved With Compassion

How can we grow in this kind of love? By taking lessons from Jesus. According to Matthew 14:14 NKJV, when **He saw a great multitude...He was moved with compassion for them, and healed their sick.**

Notice that Jesus wasn't moved with compassion until He *saw* the multitudes. What you see will affect your heart. There have been times in prayer when I've been praying for a move of God. Suddenly, the Lord allowed my heart to see the multitudes. I could see their faces. I could see their clothes. I could hear the cry of their hearts and I could see the longing in their eyes. When I saw them, I was moved with compassion so deeply that I could hardly stand it.

It was at that very point that my prayer was the most effective, because I began to pick up their cries and ask God for light on their behalf. I began to pray for laborers for them. I don't mean that someone stood up in a church service and said, "Please pray this after me. 'Dear heavenly Father, we ask You to send laborers....'" Those repeat-after-me prayers are nice to help you get started, but supplication and intercession are much deeper than that.

Lamentations 3:51 says, **Mine eye affecteth mine heart.** So, what you see really does affect your heart. It will make it dull, or it will make it sharp. How sharp is your heart? Do you want to get sharper? If so, sharpen up what you're allowing your eyes to see.

I enjoy browsing through magazines to get decorating ideas, but some of them have a lot of smut in them. There are times when I pick up a magazine and the Holy Spirit says, *You don't need that.* I listen to Him, because I want to guard my heart. If you'll guard your eyes, within two weeks you'll find yourself more spiritually sensitive.

We all want to have a sensitive heart before the Lord. Even people in the secular world are talking about how we have become desensitized by what we see with our eyes—even if what we see is fiction.

That's a bad state of affairs for people in the world, but it's critical for Christians who are supposed to be led by their hearts. Am I opposed to television and movies? I'm opposed to anything that desensitizes our hearts and makes us fumble when trying to move in compassion.

"Violence and immorality don't bother me," I've heard people say. If that's true, and they don't bother you, then you're in worse condition than you think. Your heart has grown so seared and calloused that what you see doesn't bother you. What you see on television doesn't bother you. What you see at the movies doesn't bother you. Neither does real life bother you. You have built such a wall around your heart that you can stand to see a lost and dying world, and you aren't moved with compassion. Your heart is far away from God.

Don't boast that things don't bother you; repent of it.

Sure, I know the movie you just watched wasn't real. But there are people being shot and killed every day. There are people who are starving to death, and they'll still go on crying. While you are being entertained, the unsaved are taking another step closer to hell.

That's why we need to guard our eyes and our hearts— so when we see the multitudes, we'll feel something real.

Right now, you may be realizing that your heart has grown calloused. You may be wondering what you can do about it. Quit looking at those things, and start spending more time with God in prayer, worship and the Word. Eventually, all those layers of skin over your soul will begin to peel away. You'll become thin-skinned. If you're going to be effective in the kingdom of God, that's the way you have to be. You need to be so sensitive that anything ungodly bothers you.

A friend of ours used to work in the ministry, but he moved to another state where he worked out in the world again. He'd gotten used to not smelling cigarette smoke and hearing off-color jokes. When he went back to it, he no longer had a tolerance for it. It really disturbed him.

Don't let your heart get used to worldliness. Let it be repulsive to you every time you see and hear it. Don't be repulsed by the people. Love the people, but despise the sin.

Pray To Experience the Love

One sure way you can grow in love is by praying to experience it. We know we can do that scripturally because the apostle Paul prayed that way for the members of the Ephesian church.

> I bow my knees before the Father of our Lord Jesus Christ.
>
> May you be rooted deep in love and founded securely on love, that you may have the power and be strong to apprehend and grasp with all the saints [God's devoted people, the experience of that love] what is the breadth and length and height and depth [of it];
>
> [That you may really come] to know [practically, through experience for yourselves] the love of Christ, which far surpasses mere knowledge [without experience]; that you may be filled [through all your being] unto all the fullness of God.
>
> EPHESIANS 3:14,17-19 AMP

If you want God's love to increase in your heart, pray this prayer for yourself every day: "God, I want to know the love of Christ which passes knowledge." In other words, "I don't want to just know it in my mind. I want to experience it in my heart."

Over the years, I've found that there are a lot of Christians in other countries who haven't had a fraction of the teaching that we have had here in America. Yet, they know by experience what we know only by precept. Which is better? Experience.

Another good prayer you can pray for yourself is Philippians 1:9 AMP: **And this I pray: that your love may abound yet more and more and extend to its fullest development in knowledge and all keen insight [that your love may display itself in greater depth of acquaintance and more comprehensive discernment].**

The Bible says in Romans 5:5, you already have the love of God shed abroad in your heart by the Holy Ghost, so there's no point in praying for God to give you His love. But you can pray for that love to abound. You can pray for it to come forth from you more and more!

Another Scripture that helps me focus on the love of God is Romans 12:15: **Rejoice with them that do rejoice, and weep with them that weep.**

I also like the attitude of love expressed in 1 Corinthians 9:19-22 which says,

> **For though I be free from all men, yet have I made myself servant unto all, that I might gain the more.**
>
> **And unto the Jews I became as a Jew, that I might gain the Jews; to them that are under the law, as under the law, that I might gain them that are under the law; To them that are without law, as without law, (being not without**

law to God, but under the law to Christ,) that I might gain them that are without law.

To the weak became I as weak, that I might gain the weak: I am made all things to all men, that I might by all means save some.

The verse that is most amazing to me is Romans 9:3. There Paul says, **For I could wish that myself were accursed from Christ for my brethren, my kinsmen according to the flesh.** I can hardly believe that anyone could love this much. What Paul said overwhelms me. He said, "If my kinsmen could be saved, I'd wish myself to be accursed. I want them to be saved so badly that I'd trade places with them." Would you be willing to give up your salvation for someone else? I've never loved like that, but Paul did. That's a very high degree of love.

Thank God, Paul didn't have to trade places with his Jewish brethren because Jesus did it. Jesus is our most amazing example of love. When I think of what He did, everything else is dwarfed. Our challenge is to be fed by His love.

The Bible says that He made Himself of no reputation. Honestly, that's one of the hardest things for us to sacrifice. Yet that is what love compelled Jesus to do: He made Himself of no reputation, and took upon Himself the form of a servant. He was made in the likeness of men. He humbled Himself and became obedient unto death, even death on the cross. (Phil. 2:7,8.)

Jesus was in high and lofty heaven at the right hand of the throne of God. But when He looked down upon fallen man, thank God, He didn't say, "Tsk, tsk, Father. Look what has become of our prized creation. Isn't it a terrible shame? Something ought to be done."

No. He didn't just stand up in heaven and watch as we were groping around in darkness. The Bible says that it was God's love that compelled Him to send His only begotten Son to walk with fallen man. He lived on an earth that was in its fallen condition. He had been the God of the ages, and there was nothing to confine Him. He was eternal. Yet He put Himself into a body, and He'll be in that body throughout all eternity. He forever identified Himself with us.

That's what an intercessor does. He identifies with the one in need. He makes their needs his own. Many times when I'm praying for souls, I actually feel lost. Sometimes I hear myself saying, "Oh, I'm lost. Lost." Well, I'm not lost. I'm born-again and baptized in the Holy Spirit. But when I'm praying, I'll feel like I'm sliding into hell. That is what gives me such a burden for souls.

We had an interesting prayer meeting recently. We were praying for a particular minister, and we reached a certain place in the prayer and realized we couldn't continue. It was as if we were on a treadmill waiting to go somewhere. All of a sudden, we realized that it was because we had identified the problem. The Lord showed us that the man we were praying for felt that he couldn't go on. What did we do? We prayed him through.

There was a man named Hudson Taylor, who was one of the best missionaries who ever lived. What a champion of the field! Yet people thought he was strange. He loved the Chinese people, and he identified with them. A lot of missionaries tried to act superior to the people, but not Hudson Taylor. He dressed like them. He wore a pigtail. He humbled himself and won many souls in China.

Jesus humbled Himself, and then He humbled Himself even further. He took the punishment that should have come to us. Only love will do that. Because of love, Jesus became the greatest Intercessor of all.

To Fall Upon

One of the Hebrew words for intercession comes from the root word *paga*, and it means "to impinge; by importunity to cause to fall upon; to make intercession, entreat, lay, lied upon."[2]

I thought about that definition during the Iraqi war when I read an account of a man who fell on top of a group of children while trying to protect them during an attack. Despite his efforts, they all died; but it was still a very accurate portrayal of intercession, because intercession is one person laying his life on the line for another.

In real intercessory prayer, one person will spiritually fall on another, putting themselves between the danger and the loved one. You come between that person and danger—often endangering yourself. You don't even think of yourself, because you're doing it for love's sake. Do you see why you must have love and compassion to pray this prayer? No one will put their own life on the line for a wrong motive.

In the Old Testament, an excellent example of intercession is found in Genesis 18:17. It is the account of Abraham pleading for Sodom and Gomorrah. The Lord says, **Shall I hide from Abraham that thing which I do?**

That question was a clear sign that Abraham was God's friend. He must have been, because Abraham said the most astounding thing to God.

> **And Abraham came near and said, "Would You also destroy the righteous with the wicked? Suppose there were fifty righteous within the city; would You also destroy the place and not spare it for the fifty righteous that were in it?**
>
> **"Far be it from You to do such a thing as this, to slay the righteous with the wicked, so that the righteous should be as the wicked; far be it from You! Shall not the Judge of all the earth do right?"**
>
> GENESIS 18:23-25 NKJV

You can't talk to God like that unless you're His friend. It would be presumptuous. Doesn't it sound arrogant? As though he were challenging God? **Shall not the Judge of all the earth do right?**

God wasn't offended. He loves it when someone prays from his heart this way. He enjoys seeing His people take their place in relationship with Him. Beware, though, that you don't presume on that relationship because you heard someone else pray that way. Don't just mock that prayer.

Abraham's prayer sprang spontaneously from a deep relationship with God. Abraham was willing to put his own life on the line, and he was willing to put God's reputation and character on the line. You can't do one without the other. You can't put God's character on the line without putting your life on the line. It's serious business.

Sin Provokes God

Why did Abraham have to take this risk and pray this bold prayer of intercession? These verses tell us why. And the Lord said,

> **"Because the outcry against Sodom and Gomorrah is great, and because their sin is very grave, I will go down now and see whether they have done altogether according to the outcry against it that has come to Me; and if not, I will know."**
>
> GENESIS 18:20,21 NKJV

God said that a cry had gone up from Sodom and Gomorrah. Do you remember in Genesis 4 when Cain killed Abel? God came down and said that Cain's brother's blood cried to Him. In both the murder of Abel and the cry coming from Sodom and Gomorrah, there were cries for judgment.

Sin provokes God. It always has, and it always will. It is provoking Him today. I sometimes like to tease and provoke my husband, but there is a point where he says, "Enough!" That's the way God is with sin.

The sin of the people was crying out for judgment in Sodom and Gomorrah. They were making merry, having fun and doing heinous things. They were goading God, just seeing how far they could push Him. You and I are living in a wonderful day of grace where it seems you can push Him a little further. But God hates sin. Eventually, judgment will come. Just on the ungodly? No. Judgment comes upon born-again people as well. It will strike their flesh.

Those people in Sodom and Gomorrah weren't purposely calling on God for judgment. They weren't crying out, "God, judge us!" What they were doing was sinning, and sin called for a response from God—and that response was not a blessing.

People bring judgment on themselves. Of course, they don't say, "Judge me with sickness." No one says, "Judge me with disaster." Nations don't say, "Judge me with war." But they provoke God and bring it on themselves. They have overridden their conscience. They have overridden the warnings.

Sodom and Gomorrah was a good example of that. God was so provoked that He was getting ready to rain hellfire and brimstone down on them. Yet, the Bible says that God wouldn't hide from Abraham what He was going to do. Have you ever wondered why He didn't just go ahead and destroy Sodom and Gomorrah and tell Abraham afterward? Because He knew that Abraham would intercede, and that's exactly what God wanted him to do.

Notice that Abraham didn't approach the news about Sodom and Gomorrah from a lofty and self-righteous position. He didn't say, "Aren't they terrible? Get 'em God! I've heard about them for years. Seems to me like You ought to burn them good."

Abraham didn't say that. Rather than standing beside God in the place of judgment, he stood with the very ones who had provoked God. He placed himself right in the middle of their iniquity, knowing full well that God wouldn't do a thing until Abraham got out of the way.

Intercession isn't just pleading for needs to be met and for a move of God. It has more to do with judgment. Intercession means you step where the hammer is going to fall. Sometimes that means putting yourself on the line.

Notice that Abraham used his righteousness on behalf of the unrighteous. Isn't that amazing? God would spare them for the sake of the righteous, not for their own sake. Are you beginning to see why it's so important that we as Christians are here on earth? There are people everywhere who are provoking God. God needs us to use our right standing with Him on their behalf so He won't have to destroy them.

Moses Stood in the Gap

There is another picture of true intercession in Exodus 32. This time it is Moses who stands in the gap between the unrighteous and judgment. It hadn't been long since God brought the children of Israel out of Egypt with great miracles. God spared nothing to get them out, yet they quickly sinned by building a golden calf and worshipping it. They said, "This is the god that brought us up out of Egypt."

In verse 7, we see that God was so angry that He wouldn't even claim that the people were His own. He called them *Moses'* people.

> And the Lord said unto Moses, Go, get thee down; for thy people, which thou broughtest out of the land of Egypt, have corrupted themselves: They have turned aside quickly out of the way which I commanded them: they have made them a molten calf, and have worshipped it, and have sacrificed thereunto, and said, These be thy gods, O Israel, which have brought thee up out of the land of Egypt.
>
> And the Lord said unto Moses, I have seen this people, and, behold, it is a stiffnecked people: Now therefore let me alone, that my wrath may wax hot against them, and that I may consume them: and I will make of thee a great nation.

> EXODUS 32:7-10

If God offered to kill off all the competition and make a great nation out of you, would He have to tell you to leave Him alone? He wanted Moses to step out of the way and let Him judge these people. Sad to say, most of us would have let Him do it.

In verse 10, God says, **Let me alone, that my wrath may wax hot against them.** This implies that God could only bring judgment if Moses would leave Him alone. What did Moses do? He started talking, and he threw those people right back in the lap of God.

Verse 32 shows Moses as a real intercessor. He said, **Yet now, if thou wilt forgive their sin—and if not, blot me, I pray thee, out of thy book which thou hast written.** Moses did exactly what Paul talked about when he said he would willingly give up his own salvation to see the Israelites saved. Moses told God, "If You take them, just wipe my name out of the Book of Life. I'm going with them. If You want them, You'll have to take me, too."

If Moses had sided with God, the only Israelite left would have been Moses himself. But Moses didn't side with God, he sided with the people. Moses used his righteousness to save the unrighteous. Such love!

Sometimes when we see people being so flamboyantly wicked, it's tempting for us to say, "God, they're bad! They've been disgusting me for a long time. Let the judgment begin." But that's not what Jesus has called us to do. He's called us to share His ministry of intercession and call for mercy.

Remember when the disciples told Jesus that some people wouldn't accept His ministry? They said, "Master, should we call fire down from heaven?"

Jesus answered, **You don't know what manner of spirit you are of** (Luke 9:55).

It does not impress God to call down judgment on people. It impresses God when we act like His Son and identify with ungodly people who don't deserve it. The children of Israel weren't asking for mercy. Someone had to do it for them. They were too busy dancing around a golden calf in a drunken stupor. Thank God for Moses.

Standing With the Ungodly

In Numbers 14, we see the children of Israel provoking God again. They had seen Him perform amazing miracles to bring them out of Egypt. He spared nothing in providing for them. They traveled with a cloud by day and a fire at night. Yet, they were afraid to enter the Promised Land because there were giants living in walled cities.

God was furious.

Numbers 14:11-12 records God's reaction. **And the Lord said unto Moses, How long will this people provoke me? and how long will it be ere they believe me, for all the signs which I have shewed among them? I will smite them with the pestilence, and disinherit them, and will make of thee a greater nation and mightier than they.**

Does this sound familiar? God was going to kill them and raise up a nation out of Moses. Most of us would think it was a grand opportunity. We'd say, "God, let it be so!" But Moses didn't say that because he had the heart of an intercessor. Any tendency we might have to seize on someone else's mistake, or glory in someone's failure, is the furthest thing from intercession.

What a man Moses was! The Bible calls him the meekest man who ever lived. It takes meekness to do what he did. If there's any pride in you at all, you'll never become an intercessor like Moses was.

Are you getting a picture of what intercession looks like? You're not standing for the innocent. You're not just standing for a sweet lady whom the Devil has attacked with sickness. You're standing for a person who is estranged from God. A person who has provoked God. A person who is not in relationship with God.

That's intercession.

Searching for an Intercessor

The Bible reveals that God desperately desires people who will pray such intercessory prayers. He is looking hard for them. Ezekiel 22 makes that clear. There, we see Israel in a mess. They have really provoked God.

> Her priests have violated my law, and have profaned mine holy things: they have put no difference between the holy and profane, neither have they shewed difference between the unclean and the clean, and have hid their eyes from my sabbaths, and I am profaned among them.

Her princes in the midst thereof are like wolves ravening the prey, to shed blood, and to destroy souls, to get dishonest gain. And her prophets have daubed them with untempered mortar, seeing vanity, and divining lies unto them, saying, Thus saith the Lord God, when the Lord hath not spoken.

The people of the land have used oppression, and exercised robbery, and have vexed the poor and needy: yea, they have oppressed the stranger wrongfully.

EZEKIEL 22:26-29

These people have cried out to God for judgment. Their sin provoked God day and night. So, what was God's response? Did He rush out at the first opportunity to kill them? We find His response in verse 30: **And I sought for a man among them, that should make up the hedge, and stand in the gap before me for the land, that I should not destroy it: but I found none.**

God's response to their atrocities was to actively look for someone to use their righteousness to stand in the gap. He didn't just say, "It would be nice if someone showed up to plead on these people's behalf." No, God went looking. "I sought for a man...."

Have you ever sought for something? Like your wallet, or your car keys? You go through every cupboard. You look under every sofa cushion. Then you start your search all over again.

That's the way God looked for someone to stand in the gap for these people. He looked far and wide. But the sad truth was, "I found none." What happened as a result?

159

Therefore have I poured out mine indignation upon them; I have consumed them with the fire of my wrath: their own way have I recompensed upon their heads, saith the Lord God (v.31).

God never said, "Wow, wasn't that fun?" Consuming those people wasn't what He wanted to do. It only happened because no one cared enough to intercede.

Look at what He said in Ezekiel 33:11: **Say unto them, As I live, saith the Lord God, I have no pleasure in the death of the wicked; but that the wicked turn from his way and live: turn ye, turn ye from your evil ways; for why will ye die, O house of Israel?**

God doesn't enjoy destroying His creation. That's not the nature of our Father. He is love and He delights in mercy. (Micah 7:18.)

Characteristics of Intercession

In Isaiah 43:25-26, we are given two important characteristics of intercession.

I, even I, am he that blotteth out thy transgressions for mine own sake, and will not remember thy sins.

Put me in remembrance: let us plead together: declare thou, that thou mayest be justified.

The first characteristic of intercession is that the intercessor puts God in remembrance of His Word. The second characteristic is that the intercessor pleads with God. This kind of pleading isn't an unworthy begging. It's the plea before a judge and jury, made by an attorney who represents a person charged with a crime.

If you'll study the intercession of Moses, you'll see how he pled his case before God. His plea is recorded in Exodus 32:11-13.

> **And Moses besought the Lord his God, and said, Lord, why doth thy wrath wax hot against thy people, which thou hast brought forth out of the land of Egypt with great power, and with a mighty hand?**

> **Wherefore should the Egyptians speak, and say, For mischief did he bring them out, to slay them in the mountains, and to consume them from the face of the earth? Turn from thy fierce wrath, and repent of this evil against thy people.**

> **Remember Abraham, Isaac, and Israel, thy servants, to whom thou swarest by thine own self, and saidst unto them, I will multiply your seed as the stars of heaven, and all this land that I have spoken of will I give unto your seed, and they shall inherit it for ever.**

Look again at verse 13. What is Moses asking God to do there? He's asking Him to *remember*. He is putting the Lord in remembrance of His Word. You can't put God in remembrance of something if you don't know what He said. That's why it's crucial for an intercessor to know the Word of God.

Obviously, Moses made a very strong case, because after his closing arguments, the Bible says, **The Lord repented of the evil which he thought to do unto his people** (v. 14).

Moses made another strong case in Numbers 14:17-20. Look at how he pled with the Lord there.

> **And now, I beseech thee, let the power of my Lord be great, according as thou hast spoken, saying, The Lord is longsuffering, and of great mercy, forgiving iniquity and transgression, and by no means clearing the guilty, visiting the iniquity of the fathers upon the children unto the third and fourth generation.**

> **Pardon, I beseech thee, the iniquity of this people according unto the greatness of thy mercy, and as thou hast forgiven this people, from Egypt even until now.**

> **And the Lord said, I have pardoned according to thy word.**

The Lord pardoned the Israelites' sin in this instance because Moses reminded Him of the covenant He'd made with them. He based his plea on God's blood-sworn oath to His people. That's what we do, too. We build our case on the blood of Jesus and the Word of the living God.

But I want you to notice, even though the Lord had given His Word and Moses reminded Him of it, God did not say to Moses, "I have pardoned according to My Word." No, He said, "Moses, I have pardoned according to *thy* word." It was the word of a man who dared to stand in the gap for his nation that saved the day.

Like Moses, you and I are living in days of judgment. The only reason that cities, peoples and tribes of all the nations of the world would see heaven instead of hell is because God is still looking for men and women who will stand in the gap.

We're going to see some ugly things in the world in days to come. We've already seen some. During the war with Iraq, I noticed bumper stickers that said, "Nuke them." That wasn't the cry of God's heart. He was looking for men and women who would cry, "O God, in Your judgment upon that nation, remember mercy. Remember the innocent people there."

God is searching throughout the earth for the faith-filled cry of love.

Let Him hear your voice.

10

Watching in the Spirit

Take ye heed, watch and pray; for ye
know not when the time is. And what
I say unto you I say unto all, Watch.

MARK 13:33,37

"Why do bad things happen to good people?"

You often hear that question asked in Christian circles today. It's been answered many ways. Whole books have been written about it. Yet I've never heard anyone give what I believe to be the most accurate answer. So I'll give it to you right here.

The reason bad things happen to good people, the reason the Devil is so often able to get into our churches to kill, steal and destroy is this: The Church has neglected to watch and pray.

"But wait a minute," someone might say, "we have prayer meetings in our church. We do a lot of praying!"

That may be. But how much watching do you do?

In most cases, the answer to that question would be another question, and it would sound something like this: "Well... uh... that depends. What do you mean by watching?"

Watching is the very first step to Spirit-led prayer. It is praying to pray. It is tuning in to God and purposely searching out the promptings of His Spirit. It is looking for His leadings so you can follow them and pray about things of which you have no natural knowledge.

Let's say, for example, that you sense a leading of the Lord to spend some time in prayer for your church one night. You might have no idea when you begin praying that a lady from your church is in danger. But as you just worship and wait on the Lord, watching attentively for His leading, He alerts you to that danger so you can take care of it in prayer.

Over and over, He keeps bringing that lady's face to your mind. He brings Scriptures to your heart to pray over her. You might be unaware of the exact nature of the danger, but you sense an uneasiness about her in your heart. So, in simple obedience, you just hold her before the Lord and pray in tongues until you sense a peaceful release on the inside.

Later you find out that on the very night you were praying, that precious Christian sister narrowly escaped a deadly automobile accident.

That is what it means to watch and pray.

166

Of course, you can't do that unless the Holy Spirit helps you. But I can assure you, if you are a born-again, Holy Ghost-baptized believer and you set yourself to watch and pray—help you He will! How? By doing exactly what Jesus said He would do in John 16:13-14 AMP.

> When He, the Spirit of Truth (the truth-giving Spirit) comes, He will guide you into all the Truth—the whole, full truth. For He will not speak His own message—on His own authority—but He will tell whatever He hears [from the Father, He will give the message that has been given to Him] and He will announce and declare to you the things that are to come—that will happen in the future.

> He will honor and glorify Me, because He will take of (receive, draw upon) what is Mine and will reveal (declare, disclose, transmit) it to you.

One reason the Holy Spirit is so eager to help us watch is because that's what He is doing. He is constantly watching over the world, longing to move on it in power and carry out the will of God. But He cannot do that apart from the prayers of the body of Christ. So He is ever ready to help us watch and pray.

Actually, the Holy Spirit Himself is the great Watchman. But we, too, have been appointed spiritual watchers. The Bible actually calls us that. Although we have some ideas about what the job of a watchman is, the very best picture of it can be found in the Old Testament. We see there that in the early days of Israel, they built huge walls around their cities to protect them. Watchmen were assigned to various places on the wall. Their responsibility was to watch for any significant development and cry out about what they saw.

If the city's own warriors were returning from a victorious battle, bringing with them great gain and spoil from their conquered foe, the watchmen would cry out and the city gates would be opened so they could come in. If the watchmen saw signs of danger, they would sound an alarm as it approached. If an attacker shot a flaming arrow into the wall, the watchmen's job was to pour water over it to douse the fire.

What those watchmen did on physical walls, you and I are to do on the spiritual walls where we are assigned. As we stand at our spiritual stations, we are to look into the realm of the spirit and respond to what we see. Some of what we see will be good. We'll see, for example, the promises of God. We'll see the good things He has planned for His Church.

When we see those things, we are to do what those in Isaiah 62 did. The Lord said of them, **I have set watchmen upon your walls, O Jerusalem, who will never hold their peace day or night; you who [are His servants and by your prayers] put the Lord in remembrance [of His promises], keep not silence, and give Him no rest until He establishes Jerusalem and makes it a praise in the earth** (Isaiah 62: 6,7 AMP).

When you watch in the spirit and see that God wants to establish something, like a glorious church, your job as a watcher is to give Him no rest about it. Keep not silent. Put Him in remembrance of His promises. That's what He wants you to do.

At other times on your watch, the Holy Spirit may reveal fiery darts being launched against individuals, families, ministries, cities, states, governments or nations. When that happens, your job is to pour the water of the Spirit and the Word over those situations. Your job is to yield to the promptings of the Holy Ghost and quench those darts before they ever hit their mark.

A New Testament Lesson on Watching

Speaking of fiery darts, let's look now at the passage in Ephesians 6 where that phrase is used. It gives us some very important information about watching.

> Finally, my brethren, be strong in the Lord, and in the power of his might. Put on the whole armour of God, that ye may be able to stand against the wiles of the Devil.
>
> For we wrestle not against flesh and blood, but against principalities, against powers, against the rulers of the darkness of this world, against spiritual wickedness in high places.
>
> Wherefore take unto you the whole armour of God, that ye may be able to withstand in the evil day, and having done all, to stand. Stand therefore, having your loins girt about with truth, and having on the breastplate of righteousness; And your feet shod with the preparation of the gospel of peace; Above all, taking the shield of faith,

wherewith ye shall be able to quench all the fiery darts of the wicked.

And take the helmet of salvation, and the sword of the Spirit, which is the word of God: Praying always with all prayer and supplication in the Spirit, and watching thereunto with all perseverance and supplication for all saints.

Ephesians 6:10-18

You can see by these verses that God desires to grant us a place in the spirit where we can resist demonic forces and thwart their plans. In fact, Paul actually lists four levels of demonic forces God has given us the authority to deal with: principalities, powers, rulers of the darkness of this world and wicked spirits in heavenly places.

Let me make one thing clear, however. We are not trying to defeat these forces. Jesus has already defeated them. He spoiled principalities and powers at His resurrection and made an open spectacle of them. Now He reigns **far above all principality, and power, and might, and dominion** (Ephesians 1:21).

Our job is simply to enforce their defeat.

Let me give you an example that may help you see the difference. One morning recently, I walked out into my front yard, and there was a policeman driving by my house. I thought it was wonderful that he was patrolling in our neighborhood. He was out enforcing the law that has already been established.

In a similar way, that's what we do. We patrol and watch to make sure the Devil doesn't get a foothold somewhere. We aren't out to establish the law, but to enforce what Jesus has already established. That's why it's so important that we put on the whole armor of God when we stand against those demons to enforce their defeat. It's His power and authority we're wielding against them, not our own.

Some Christians have tried to slip out of that responsibility. They want to just ignore those devils and hope they'll go away. But that's not what God tells us to do. He doesn't tell us to pretend they aren't there. He tells us to put on our armor and oppose them.

Secrets of Ruling and Reigning

I have to be honest with you though. When you're dealing with spiritual things, you have to put first things first. Before you're going to have much success exercising your authority over devils and ruling over them, you first have to exercise your authority and rule over your own flesh. That means you must watch over yourself.

For instance, you must make yourself walk in love. Nobody else can rule over you and make you be kind and gentle and patient. You have to do it yourself. If you don't rule over yourself, then you will never rule, as the Bible says, over ten cities. How could you be entrusted over kingdoms if you refuse to rule over yourself?

It's silly when a believer, who yells at her husband, gets offended with people and gossips about her neighbor and later stands up in prayer and takes authority over some devil that's ruling a nation. Do you think that devil is going to listen to her? No, he won't. Why should a major national devil run from a believer who's being whipped by her own flesh and also by minor, local devils of anger, offense and gossip?

Why would the Holy Spirit open that realm to someone like that? He wouldn't. Remember what the landlord in Jesus' parable said to his servant who had dealt wisely with the money he had been given. He said, **Thou good and faithful servant; thou hast been faithful over a few things, I will make thee ruler over many things** (Matthew 25:21).

That principle is repeated in Proverbs 12:24 KJV: **The hand of the diligent shall bear rule.**

If you will be diligent to watch over yourself, to keep yourself in the love of God and walk holy and upright before Him, then He will promote you. He'll enlarge your territory to include other believers and the realm of the church. He'll give you more to watch over. He'll also take you to higher places in the realm of this spirit so you can see what you need to see.

If you're diligent there, He'll enlarge your territory some more to include nations. And He'll take you even higher in the spirit so that you can watch from there.

It's a step-by-step process that's captured perfectly in Zechariah 3. There we see the heavenly ordination of Joshua, the high priest. He is actually standing with the angels before the throne of God. In verse 7 in *The Amplified Bible*, God addresses Joshua and says, **Thus says the Lord of hosts: If**

you will walk in My ways and keep My charge, then also you shall rule My house and have charge of my courts, and I will give you access [to My presence] and places to walk among these who stand here.

Notice that the first thing the Lord told him was to **walk in My ways and keep My charge.** That's the first thing we all have to do. He was telling Joshua that, first and foremost, he had to rule over himself to ensure that he would always walk in the ways of the Lord.

Second, after ruling over himself, the Lord told Joshua that he would rule over God's house. Third, He said that Joshua would have charge of God's courts. How was God going to give Joshua that ability? By giving him places to walk in the Spirit. By giving him access to heavenly realms to work right alongside the angels.

Watchers in Action

If you want to see a scriptural example of some high-level watchers in action, read Daniel 4. There we see Nebuchadnezzar, king of Babylon, describing a dream God had given him. The dream was a warning, and in it he saw a tree that grew and reached to the heavens.

Its leaves were fair and its fruit abundant, and in it was food for all. The living creatures of the field found shade under it, and the birds of the sky dwelt in its branches, and all flesh fed from it.

I saw in the visions of my head [as I lay] on my bed, and behold a watcher, a holy one, came down from Heaven. He cried aloud [with might] and said, Hew down the tree and cut off its branches, shake off its leaves and scatter its fruit; let the living creatures flee from under it and the fowls from its branches.

Nevertheless leave the stump of its roots in the earth, bound with a band of iron and bronze, in the midst of the tender grass of the field. Let him be wet with the dew of the heavens, and let him share the lot of the living creatures in the grass of the earth; Let his nature and understanding be changed from a man's, and let a beast's nature...be given him, and let seven times [or years] pass over him.

This sentence is by the decree of the [heavenly] watchers, and the decision is by the word of the holy ones, to the intent that the living may know that the Most High [God] rules.

DANIEL 4:12-16 AMP

When Nebuchadnezzar called for Daniel (who was also a watcher), Daniel revealed the interpretation of his dream. He told Nebuchadnezzar that the tree represented the king himself. He warned him that unless he changed his ways, he would be mentally deranged for seven years. He would be driven from the palace and live like an animal.

But what I want you to notice is this. It was not God Himself who spoke that decree in Nebuchadnezzar's dream. It was spoken by the watchers. Who are these heavenly watchers? Verse 17 calls them *holy ones* and uses the same word that in other places is translated *saints*. They are the people of God who have been given charge of God's house and His courts. They are the people who rule through prayer in heavenly places.

Another thing I want you to notice is the fact that these watchers weren't making requests of God; they were making declarations for Him. They were announcing His decree about the situation. They were making commands and saying "This is how things are going to be."

That's the way it is with watching. Sometimes you'll pray, and sometimes you'll say. If you doubt the scriptural propriety of that, read Mark 11:22-24. There Jesus said, **Whosoever shall say unto this mountain, Be thou removed, and be thou cast into the sea; and shall not doubt in his heart, but shall believe that those things which he saith shall come to pass, he shall have whatsoever he saith. Therefore...What things soever ye desire, when ye pray, believe that ye receive them, and ye shall have them.**

Clearly, there is power in praying, and there is power in saying. So when you're watching, you will be led by the Holy Spirit to do both.

In Daniel 5, you'll find another example of what can happen when a watcher declares the Word of the Lord. There, we find king Belshazzar, Nebuchadnezzar's son and heir to his throne in Babylon, feasting in his palace. In spite of the fact that Belshazzar knew about the wonders God had done during his father's reign, he had no fear of the Lord. He was so foolish and proud that, during his feast, he decided to further defile the name of the God of Israel. So he called for the gold and silver vessels that had been removed from the temple at Jerusalem, and he distributed them among his princes, wives and concubines so they could drink wine from them at his party.

When he did that, a fearsome thing happened. The fingers of a man appeared supernaturally and wrote a message on his wall. The message, which was again interpreted by Daniel, declared that Belshazzar had been found wanting, and his kingdom was going to be taken from him that very night and given to the Medes and the Persians.

Sure enough, that night Beshazzar was slain by Darius, king of the Medes, and the kingdom of Babylon fell, just as the message foretold.

In the book of Daniel, the record of this incident says nothing about the watchers. But if you'll do some further scriptural investigation, you'll find that just as before, this decree came by the mouth of a watcher—a watcher named Isaiah.

In Isaiah 21, he gives us the account of what he saw and what he said about this incident as he watched in the spirit. Keep in mind as you read it that Isaiah died many years before this ever took place.

My mind reels and wanders, horrors terrifies me. [In my mind's eye I am at the feast of Belshazzar; I see the defilement of the golden vessels taken from God's temple; I watch the handwriting appear on the wall, I know that Babylon's great king is to be slain.] The twilight I looked forward to with pleasure has been turned into fear and trembling for me.

They prepare the table, they spread the rugs, and having set the watchers [the revellers take no other precaution], they eat, they drink. Arise, you princes, and oil your shields [for your deadly foe is at the gates]!

For thus has the Lord said to me, Go, set [yourself as] a watchman, let him declare what he sees. And when he sees a troop, horsemen in pairs, a troop of donkeys and a troop of camels, he shall listen diligently, very diligently.

And the watchman cried like a lion: O Lord, I stand continually on the watchtower in the daytime, and I am set in my station every night through.

ISAIAH 21:2-6 AMP

Isn't that amazing? The Spirit of God gave Isaiah a place to stand, pray and make decrees about something that was going to happen in his nation—not next week or next month, but in the next century.

Truly, our God is an awesome God!

Watching Can Make the Crucial Difference

⟨⟨⟩⟩

Although I certainly don't count myself among the ranks of watchers like Isaiah, I have had some interesting experiences while watching in prayer. One in particular impressed upon me how very crucial watching can be.

It happened some years ago when my husband, Mac, was in Peru on a mission trip. I was watching in the spirit and praying for him one day when I saw (not with my physical eyes, but with the eyes of my spirit) a demon power of death that was going to try to move in on him.

To some people that may sound like a frightening thing to see. But I wasn't afraid. The fact that the Holy Spirit enabled me to see it was proof that He was already on the case. He had already taken hold in this fight, and He always enables us to win.

So I didn't get in a panic and start flailing around in the flesh, binding and loosing anything I could think of. No, I just kept watching and praying, waiting for the leading of the Lord. I've learned you can't deal with demons or anything else without an unction from God. That's why people get discouraged, because they try to do something in the flesh and nothing happens.

Of course, I did the things that you can do without an unction. I pled the blood of Jesus over Mac. I prayed the Word of God over him. And I kept on watching.

As each day passed, I was more aware in my heart that something was up. Then when I woke up one night and began praying over him, the Lord spoke to me. He said, *I want you to deal with this spirit of death when you preach in church on Wednesday night.*

I don't mind telling you, I argued with the Lord. I had no intention of mentioning that spirit to the church. I said, "Lord, I don't want to do that. There will be baby Christians in the service. Can you imagine their reaction if I announce that a devil is going to try and kill their pastor?"

Unmoved by my protests, the Lord instructed me to do it anyway. He said that we were going to win this battle, and He wanted the whole congregation to share in the reward.

Sure enough, on Wednesday night God gave us the unction to deal with that spirit. I'll never forget that service because I had the strangest sensation while we prayed. I felt like my body was on fire. I burned during the whole service.

Although the spirit of death had been dealt with, I continued to watch and pray during the next several days. Finally, in the early hours of the morning on Sunday, I bolted up in bed with the unction of God flowing through me like a river. I declared, "Mac's wings! Lord, You give him wings! Wheels! Wheels! It's going in! Mac, take your position of authority in the name of Jesus, and they'll get out!"

It was so amazing to me that I wrote it down word for word. That's all there was to it. After I made those declarations, the unction lifted. The next day I preached, and the following day I left for a speaking engagement in Alabama. Mac flew back into the country and met me there. When he slid into the seat next to me during a service, I hugged him and whispered, "What happened to you Sunday morning?"

"My plane crashed," he said.

Later he told me the whole story. The wheels on the plane didn't come down during the landing. When that happened, everyone on board froze in fear. Even the pilots were so paralyzed by fear that they couldn't move. The first thing you do if an airplane lands on its belly is shut off the engines, because the plane can explode in flames. But the pilots froze, so Mac took authority and said in a loud voice, "Everybody get up and get out!"

The engines were running, and there was gasoline all over the runway. The officials said it was a miracle that the airplane didn't blow up and burn. When I heard that, I thought about how my body had burned during the Wednesday night service when we had prayed, and I knew why that miracle had happened. The Holy Ghost was on the scene of that fire before it ever started. He enabled His watchers to quench that fiery dart before it ever hit its mark!

In Dangerous Days

Many times Christians are amazed when I tell that story, but they shouldn't be. This is just bottom-line Christianity. This is how God meant for us to live—especially in these last days.

Because we have reached the culmination of this age, we are living in the most dangerous of times. Jesus Himself warned us about them. He said they would be marked by wars, rumors of wars, famines, calamities, earthquakes and persecutions. So in Mark, He gave us this charge:

> Be on your guard (constantly alert) and watch and pray, for you do not know when the time will come.
>
> It is like a man (already) going on a journey; when he leaves home he puts his servants in charge, each with his particular task, and he gives orders to the doorkeeper to be constantly alert and on the watch. Therefore watch— give strict attention, be cautious and alert—for you do not know when the Master of the house is coming, in the evening, or at midnight, or at cockcrowing, or in the morning.
>
> [Watch, I say] lest He come suddenly and unexpectedly and find you asleep. And what I say to you I say to everybody: (Give strict attention, be cautious, active, alert, and) watch!
>
> MARK 13:33-37 AMP

The original word translated *watch* there means "to be sleepless." God is warning the Church not to be caught asleep in these last days.

While that warning is important for every believer, it is especially crucial for ministers. They are under a special mandate to watch and pray. You can see that in Hebrews 13:17 AMP.

> Obey your spiritual leaders and submit to them—continually recognizing their authority over you; for they are

181

constantly keeping watch over your souls and guarding your spiritual welfare, as we who will have to render an account [of their trust]. [Do your part to] let them do this with gladness, and not with sighing and groaning, for that would not be profitable to you [either].

Ministers will have to give an account of their watching over their flock. God holds them responsible spiritually for those He has given them authority over. If they'll seek Him, they'll find He also equips them for the task. He will enable them to guard the sheep under their care supernaturally. He will help them watch and pray.

Avoiding King Asa's Mistake

Some time ago in the middle of the night, I woke up with the spirit of prophesy on me. I spoke out the word of the Lord as He said, "I am setting up watchtowers all over the earth to watch in the realm of the Spirit. And I'm going to give you territories to watch."

I'm telling you, God is winding things up now. He is on a timetable, and He is using every available resource to get this end-time job done. So if you're a pray-er and you're diligent— get ready. He is going to expand your territory.

A lot of people get excited when that happens. They say, "Glory to God! The Lord gave me New Zealand!" That's wonderful, but what I said before I'm going to say again. If you don't continue to watch over yourself, the Devil will steal New Zealand from you.

Remember this: our responsibility to watch ourselves doesn't decrease as our territory increases. It increases!

That's the reason why so many pray-ers get off into flaky things of the flesh—they don't stand guard over themselves. They let their basic walk with God begin to slip. They start thinking that because they're such powerful pray-ers, they don't have to bother with being kind to people or spending time in the Word.

Don't make that mistake. No matter how much God gives you to watch over, remain diligent to watch first and foremost over yourself. One way to do that is through consecration. As I said before, in the chapter about the prayer of consecration, it doesn't happen by getting in your prayer closet one day and saying, "God, I consecrate myself to You." Consecration comes by degrees, day by day, from one week to the next.

The second thing you can do in watching over yourself is to inquire of God. Every day I ask, "Lord, what weights can I set aside so that I can be more consecrated to You?" The third thing you'll have to do is stay in the Word of God. Don't just look in your Bible to get Scriptures to pray. Read it. Meditate on it. Go to church and hear it preached. Listen to tapes by anointed men and women of God. Keep the Word of God dwelling richly in you.

What will happen if you don't? Look at the account of King Asa in 2 Chronicles 15, and you'll find out. There you'll see a picture of a man whose territory was expanded, and then he lost it all because he failed to keep watch over himself.

Asa's walk with the Lord parallels this day and hour. There were afflictions and disturbances, and nations were against nations and cities against cities. For a long time before Asa began to reign, Judah had to struggle along without the help of God because they had turned away from seeking Him. Finally, in desperation over their trouble, they cried out to God, and He responded to them through the prophet Oded.

> And when Asa heard these words, the prophecy of Oded the prophet, he took courage, and put away the abominable idols from all the land of Judah and Benjamin and from the cities which he had taken in the hill country of Ephraim, and he repaired the altar [of burnt offering] of the Lord which was in front of the porch or vestibule [of the house] of the Lord.
>
> And he gathered all Judah and Benjamin and the strangers with them out of Ephraim, Manasseh and Simeon; for they came over to Asa out of Israel in large numbers, when they saw that the Lord his God was with him.
>
> 2 CHRONICLES 15:8,9 AMP

The Bible goes on to record that they sacrificed seven hundred oxen and seven hundred sheep, and they entered a covenant with God. Asa went even further and removed his mother from being queen mother, because she made an abominable image for Asherah. Wasn't that a courageous thing to do? He put God before his own mother. Then he brought back into the house of God the things that his father had dedicated, as well as those that he had dedicated. Afterwards, there was no more war for twenty years.

Proverbs 16:7 says that when a man's ways please the Lord, even his enemies are at peace with him. Asa's ways greatly pleased God. As a result, his territory was expanded. Although he was king of Judah, many people from Israel came to live under his reign. They began to migrate to him because they saw that God was with him. That's exactly what needs to happen today. Whole cities need to see that God is with us.

However, in 2 Chronicles 16, the picture changes. After twenty years, a great war raged against Asa. The king of Israel tried to take his land. Instead of seeking God as he'd done in the past, Asa sent gold and silver to another king, the king of Syria, and asked him for protection. God sent a prophet to warn Asa, but he still did not repent and seek the Lord.

I believe that the prophecy through Oded twenty years earlier warned of this tragedy. Let's look at it again.

> **The Spirit of God came upon Azariah the son of Oded, and he went out to meet Asa...and all Judah and Benjamin: The Lord is with you while you are with Him. If you seek Him [inquiring for and of Him, craving Him as your soul's first necessity], He will be found of you; but if you [become indifferent and] forsake Him, He will forsake you.**

> 2 CHRONICLES 15 1,2 AMP

185

Twenty years before Asa turned to the arm of the flesh for help, God had warned him of things to come. The prophet had said, "Asa, if you forsake God, He will forsake you."

What happened? Why did Asa, who had turned all of Judah back to God, fail to look to Him during this time of great trouble?

I'll tell you why. He had stopped watching over himself.

There had been peace for twenty years, and Asa had been able to coast along just fine. He was no longer spiritually keen and sharp. Asa's biggest crime wasn't that he failed to watch over his territory. He could have handled the attack against his kingdom if he'd been watching over himself.

So much of our lives depends on watching and praying. Asa was not watching. He was not on guard. He was not attentive to his own spiritual condition. I believe Asa became entrapped by the business of life. Jesus warns us about that in Luke 21:34 AMP: **But take heed to yourselves and be on your guard lest your hearts be overburdened and depressed—weighed down—with the giddiness and headache and nausea of self-indulgence, drunkenness, and worldly worries and cares pertaining to (the business of) this life, and that day come upon you suddenly like a trap or a noose.**

Asa was probably busy ruling his kingdom, and he lost that sharp edge in the Spirit. After he made covenant with another king, the prophet of God spoke to him again.

For the eyes of the Lord run to and fro throughout the whole earth, to show Himself strong in behalf of those

whose heart is blameless toward Him. You have done foolishly in this; therefore from now on you shall have wars.

Then Asa was angry with the seer, and put him in prison—in the stocks—for he was enraged with him because of this. Asa oppressed some of the people at the same time.

The acts of Asa, first to last, are written in the Book of the Kings of Judah and Israel. In the thirty-ninth year of his reign Asa was diseased in his feet, until his disease became very severe; yet in his disease he did not seek the Lord, but relied on the physicians.

And Asa slept with his fathers, dying in the forty-first year of his reign.

2 CHRONICLES 15:9-13 AMP

Asa had some great victories in God early in his life. God lifted him to places of rulership. But eventually he began resting on the laurels of his former success. He didn't seek God with the same hunger he had in his early days. He failed to watch over his own heart, and that failure cost him not only his reign, it cost him his life.

Asa's story never has to be repeated in any believer's life. There is no reason for you to start in the spirit and end in the flesh. Sharpen your spiritual vision through the Word of God. Stay diligent to guard your own heart.

Watch and pray.

11

❦

Waiting on God

*But they that wait upon the Lord shall renew
their strength; they shall mount up with wings
as eagles; they shall run, and not be weary;
and they shall walk, and not faint.*

Isaiah 40:31

If you study the revivals and great moves of God in the past,
you'll find a phenomenon that is unheard of in most of
christendom today. The Bible calls it *waiting on the Lord*. The
dear old saints in those days knew how to sit down, be quiet
and wait on God. It wasn't unusual for whole congregations to
sit in a service for three hours without anyone saying a word.
Everyone was content. No one fidgeted in his or her chair. No
one stood up to prophesy.

Sadly, waiting on the Lord is almost a lost art today. But it
is a great weapon that the Church must regain and begin to use

in this hour. We need it desperately—first of all, because many believers are tired. The onslaught of the Devil in these last days is wearing out the saints.

But, thank God, we don't have to stay worn out. The Scriptures tell us that waiting on God will refresh and strengthen us. It will put us in the place of victory and blessing. If we refuse to wait, however, and push frantically on in our own strength, we'll be like the Israelites in Isaiah 30. Look what happened to them!

> **For thus said the Lord God, the Holy One of Israel, In returning, to Me and resting in Me you shall be saved; in quietness and in (trusting) confidence shall be your strength. But you would not.**
>
> **But you said, No! We will speed our own course on horses! Therefore you shall speed [in flight from your enemies]. You said, We will ride upon swift steeds [doing our own way]! Therefore shall they who pursue you be swift, so swift that one thousand of you will flee at the threat of one of them; at the threat of five you will flee till you are left like a beacon or a flagpole on top of a mountain, and like a signal on a hill.**
>
> **And therefore the Lord [earnestly] waits— expectant, looking and longing—to be gracious to you, and therefore He lifts Himself up that He may have mercy on you and show loving-kindness to you; for the Lord is a God of justice. Blessed—happy, fortunate [to be envied] are all those who [earnestly] wait for Him.**
>
> Isaiah 30:15-18 AMP

Most Christians today act just like the people in this passage. They need God's help because the Devil is closing in on them in some area of their lives. But instead of waiting on God quietly and resting in Him until the answer comes, they jump up and do a bunch of stuff in their own strength. They wear themselves out—and then lose the battle to boot!

Not only do strength, victory and blessing come to those who wait on the Lord, revelation comes too. **For since the beginning of the world men have not heard, nor perceived by the ear, neither hath the eye seen, O God, beside thee, what he hath prepared for him that waiteth for him** (Isa. 64:4).

There are secret things reserved for those who wait on God. Most people just hear those secrets secondhand from other people. But you can hear them directly from the Spirit of God if you will get in His presence—and wait.

The Bible also tells of another benefit of waiting. It says, **They shall not be ashamed that wait for me** (Isa. 49:23). If you will wait on the Lord, He will do whatever needs to be done to prepare and equip you so that you won't be ashamed when Jesus comes. You'll be ready. I don't know about you, but I want to be ready to meet Him on that day. I want to hear Him say "Well, done!" But if that's going to happen, I have some changing to do.

How will those changes be made? The Lord spoke to me about that one time. He said, *If you will give Me one thing, I can change anything about you. I can change your mind. I can change your soul. I can change your body. I can change your finances. The* one thing I need is the one thing that has been hardest for you to give—*your time.*

If God can get you to stay in His presence, He can handle any impossibility in your life. There are some people whose whole personalities need to be changed and rearranged before they can fit in the place where they have been called. If you'll sow time waiting in God's presence, you will reap those results.

Time for Everything

"But I don't have time to just wait in God's presence!"

Yes, you do. You're just spending that time doing something else. That's why, as Christians, we need to take a fresh look at the time God has given us. Sure, we have to spend time on the job and time with family and friends. We spend time shopping, cooking and cleaning. We spend time in prayer. But there are times when God simply calls us to wait on Him. If we'll trust God to order our steps and if we'll obey His promptings during the other hours of our day, when it comes time to wait, we'll be able to do it.

Ecclesiastes 3:1-14 talks about this principle.

To every thing there is a season, and a time to every purpose under the heaven: a time to be born, and a time to die; a time to plant, and a time to pluck up that which is planted; a time to kill, and a time to heal; a time to break down, and a time to build up; a time to weep, and a

time to laugh; a time to mourn, and a time to dance; a time to cast away stones, and a time to gather stones together; a time to embrace, and a time to refrain from embracing; a time to get, and a time to lose; a time to keep, and a time to cast away; a time to rend, and a time to sew; a time to keep silence, and a time to speak; a time to love, and a time to hate; a time of war, and a time of peace.

What profit hath he that worketh in that wherein he laboureth?

I have seen the travail, which God hath given to the sons of men to be exercised in it.

He hath made every thing beautiful in his time.

This Scripture points out the importance of staying in God's timing. It's possible to do the right thing but have the wrong results, simply because it wasn't God's time. If you follow God's timetable, you won't miss His plan for your life. You'll also have all that you need for whatever you encounter. Because you're at the right place at the right time, God's supply will be there for you. If you need grace, it will be multiplied to you. If you need strength, it will be multiplied to you.

It's wonderful to be on time.

Don't Miss Your Visitation

By the same token, it can really cost you when you get busy doing things by perspiration instead of inspiration and you step out of God's timing. The Bible tells about people who did that. You can read about one of them in Luke 10.

In this account, Jesus was going to visit Mary and Martha. Think about that for a minute. If Jesus were coming to your house for a visit, you could expect an experience that would take you significantly higher in the glory of God. It would be an experience that might not ever be repeated, and it certainly would never be forgotten.

Yet, Martha was so distracted with natural activities that she missed what God meant to be one of the most meaningful moments of her life. Instead of getting still and listening to what Jesus had to say that day, she got busy in the kitchen, banging around with pots and pans.

What's more, she was irritated because her sister, Mary, was just sitting at the feet of the Master like there was nothing else to do. Finally, in exasperation, she asked Jesus, **Lord, is it nothing to You that my sister has left me to serve alone? Tell her then to help me** (v. 40 AMP).

But Jesus replied, **Martha, Martha, you are anxious and troubled about many things. There is need of only one...Mary has chosen the good portion** (v. 41 AMP). Jesus was saying that at this particular time, Martha really needed only one thing—her visitation from God. If she had discerned the time properly, she would have been greatly blessed. Her timing was off.

Spiritual Traps

Once when I was visiting with a pastor who is one of the great prayer warriors of our time, she said, "I don't know what's wrong with me. I've never been so weary and faint-hearted."

The moment she said it, I knew exactly what was wrong. "Your timing is off," I said. I could say that with confidence, because I knew that we are called to walk near to Jesus in this hour—like Mary did. Exhaustion is a characteristic of Martha, who missed the time of her visitation. It is through those visitations that we are refreshed and renewed.

My friend also went on to tell me that she'd never seen such fatigue as she was seeing among the pray-ers in her church. They'd fallen into the same trap.

Did you know that there are some traps in spiritual warfare you must learn to avoid? One of those traps is failing to discern when to step out of the battle and into God's presence. Another one is failing to understand God's timing about when to use your spiritual weapons and also which one to use. You need to know when to pray in tongues and resist the Devil and when to worship God, when to confess the Word and when to plead the blood. You cannot discern those things unless you fellowship with God. One way to do that is by waiting in His presence.

Sometimes Christians get over into the darkness of spiritual warfare and don't know how to get out. When they step out of their prayer closet, instead of leaving the oppression behind, they drag it back with them into the natural realm.

There have been many times when I've been warring in the spirit, and I suddenly knew I needed to get out of the battle. I told the people in my prayer group, and they began to sing. Sometimes I sing, but often I wait on the Lord in the middle of the battle.

It's important that we not miss the time of our visitation with God, especially in the middle of battle. Brother Hagin has often told of a man who was a great and powerful pray-er, one of the greatest he'd ever seen. But the man began warring in the spirit and never laid it down. Eventually, the spiritual pressure became too much for him, and he committed suicide.

Remember, when you are praying prayers of spiritual warfare, you are wrestling with demonic powers. Will there always be demonic powers to wrestle? Yes, until Jesus returns. Do you need to wrestle with them all the time? No, you need to spend time waiting on your heavenly Father.

We are told in Psalm 37:7: **Rest in the Lord, and wait patiently for him.** Did you know it is a compliment to God when you rest in Him? You can say that you trust Him, but if you're thrashing and flailing around, your actions are speaking a louder message. What you're saying is that you have more faith in your efforts in prayer than you have in God. You're acting like the victory depends primarily on you instead of on Him.

When you stop flailing and wait on God, it suddenly becomes quite clear that the battle is the Lord's. He becomes the focus—not you. Can you defeat the Devil that way? Certainly. In Psalm 37:34 we are told, **Wait on the Lord, and keep his way, and he shall exalt thee to inherit the land: when the wicked are cut off, thou shalt see it.**

Waiting Will Set You in Motion

A lot of people confuse waiting on God with doing nothing, but they are not the same. When you wait on God, you receive His plans, plans that will put you into motion somewhere in your life. He may tell you to get out of debt. He may instruct you to bring order to your relationships. But you'll always be making progress somewhere through the instructions you receive from God.

A young woman I know traveled to Africa as a missionary some years ago. When she came home, she didn't know what to do. So she waited on the Lord and cried out to Him for direction. As she did, He spoke to her and instructed her not to settle down, get a house and buy furniture, but to live in such a way that she could pack up and leave in two weeks if necessary. She obeyed. She didn't get tied to anything that she couldn't untie in two weeks time. She didn't go into debt. For over a year she lived ready to leave.

Finally, she got a call from a friend in China who said they needed another English teacher at the university where she taught. "I don't have a degree in English," she explained. "I have a degree in medicine."

"Yes, but you *can* teach English," the friend said, "and the job is yours on one condition. You have to be here in two weeks."

Because this young missionary waited on the Lord, she didn't miss His timing for her work in China. She did exactly what is described in Psalm 40:1: **I waited patiently for the Lord; and he inclined unto me, and heard my cry.** Yes, it's exciting that God answered, but most of us skip over the first part that says, **I waited patiently for the Lord.**

If you need to be delivered out of the hand of the Devil or delivered into the perfect plan of God, ask yourself these questions. Who are you directing your cry to? To God, or to your friends?

Who have you talked to the most about your situation? Was it God? If not, your first step is to get quiet before Him. Sometimes you'll find you're so wound up that it takes time just to get quiet enough to wait. So waiting on God won't be something you can do in five minutes.

You need to get so quiet that your mind can hear what the Spirit of God is saying to your heart. It's not like He hasn't been talking to you. It's just that you haven't been able to hear Him through all the clamor in your soul. Waiting on God doesn't make Him speak louder; it stills the noise so that you can hear. The longer you wait on Him, the less distinct other people's voices and opinions become.

When you hear the instruction God gives, don't expect something flashy. Preparation for a miracle isn't usually glamorous. For instance, what was glamorous about bringing five loaves and fishes to where Jesus was preaching? Remember the story of Elisha and the widow in 2 Kings 4? There was nothing glamorous about gathering jars. It was mundane and tedious, but it was preparation for a miracle.

Psalm 46:10 says, **Be still, and know that I am God: I will be exalted among the heathen, I will be exalted in the earth. Psalm 4:4 says, Stand in awe, and sin not: commune with your own heart upon your bed, and be still.**

Do you want God to be exalted in your life? Then do what these verses say to do.

Certainly it's fun to have fun. It's great to fellowship with other believers. It's wonderful to do the work of the ministry. But there's a time to be still, a time to turn off the phone and refuse to answer the door. Nobody is more important than God.

Don't miss the time of your visitation.

Endnotes

Chapter 5

[1]Hagin, pp. 50-51.

Chapter 6

[1]Strong, "Greek," entry #154, p. 9

Chapter 9

[1]Howard.

[2]Strong, "Hebrew," entry #6293, p. 93

References

Hagin, Kenneth E. *Prevailing Prayer to Peace*. Tulsa: Faith Library Publications.

Howard, Philip E. *The Life and Diary of David Brainerd*. Ed. Jonathan Edwards. Grand Rapids: Baker Book House, 1989.

Strong, James. Strong's Exhaustive Concordance of the Bible. "Hebrew and Chaldee Dictionary." "Greek Dictionary of the New Testament." Nashville: Abingdon, 1890.

About the Authors

Lynne Hammond is a nationally known teacher and writer on the subject of prayer. Her books include, *When Healing Doesn't Come Easily, Dare to Be Free* and *The Master is Calling: Discovering the Wonders of Spirit-Led Prayer.*

She is the host and teacher for *A Call to Prayer,* a weekly European television broadcast, and occasional guest teacher on *The Winner's Way with Mac Hammond,* a national, weekly television broadcast. She also writes regular articles on the subject of prayer in *Winner's Way* magazine and publishes a newsletter called *Prayer Notes* for people of prayer. Lynne is a frequent speaker at national prayer conferences and meetings around the country.

Lynne's husband, Mac, is founder and pastor of Living Word Christian Center, a large and growing church in Minneapolis, Minnesota. Under Lynne's leadership, the prayer ministry at Living Word has become a nationally recognized model for developing effective pray-ers in the local church.

The desire of Lynne's heart is to impart the spirit of prayer to churches and nations throughout the world.

Patsy Cameneti, a RHEMA Bible Training Center graduate and former instructor, has traveled throughout the world ministering God's anointed Word in Bible schools, prayer seminars and various conferences. The focus of her ministry is to help both ministers and lay people be all that God has called them to be, as well as to be more effective in the kingdom of God. Patsy and her husband, Tony, currently reside in Padova, Italy, where their ministry in Italy and Europe is based. Tony and Patsy have two daughters, Liliana and Annalisa.

To contact Lynne Hammond or Patsy Cameneti, write:

Lynne Hammond

P.O. Box 29469

Minneapolis, MN 55429

Cameneti Ministries

P.O. Box 1880

Warren, OH 44482

Please include your prayer requests

and comments when you write.

Additional copies of this book are

available from your local bookstore.

HARRISON HOUSE

Tulsa, Oklahoma 74153

Prayer of Salvation

A born-again, committed relationship with God is the key to the victorious life. Jesus, the Son of God laid down His life and rose again so that we could spend eternity with Him in heaven and experience His absolute best on earth. The Bible says, **"For God so loved the world, that he gave his only begotten Son, that whosoever believeth in him should not perish, but have everlasting life"** (John 3:16).

It is the will of God that everyone receive eternal salvation. The way to receive this salvation is to call upon the name of Jesus and confess Him as your Lord. The Bible says, **"That if thou shalt confess with thy mouth the Lord Jesus, and shalt believe in thine heart that God hath raised him from the dead, thou shalt be saved. For whosoever shall call upon the name of the Lord shall be saved"** (Romans 10:9-10,13).

Jesus has given salvation, healing and countless benefits to all who call upon His name. These benefits can be yours if you receive Him into your heart by praying this prayer.

Heavenly Father, I come to You admitting that I am a sinner. Right now, I choose to turn away from sin, and I ask You to cleanse me of all unrighteousness. I believe that Your Son, Jesus died on the cross to take away my sins. I also believe that He rose again from the dead so that I might be justified and made righteous through faith in Him. I call upon the name of Jesus Christ to be the Savior and Lord of my life. Jesus, I choose to follow You, and ask that You fill me with the power of the Holy Spirit. I declare that right now, I am a born-again child of God. I am free from sin, and full of the righteousness of God. I am saved in Jesus' name, Amen.

If you have prayed this prayer to receive Jesus Christ as your Savior, or if this book has changed your life, we would like to hear from you. Please write us at:

Harrison House Publishers
P.O. Box 35035
Tulsa, Oklahoma 74153

You can also visit us on the web at
www.harrisonhouse.com

The Harrison House Vision

Proclaiming the truth and the power

Of the Gospel of Jesus Christ

With excellence;

Challenging Christians to

Live victoriously,

Grow spiritually,

Know God intimately.